HOW TO CHANGE HISTORY

University of Nebraska Press | Lincoln

"*How to Change History* delightfully captures the pervasive influence of the past—personal, familial, historical—on 'the temporary haven of the present.' With humor, deep insight, and keen self-scrutiny, Robin Hemley reminds us that although history can't really be changed, our understanding of it remains open to revision."
—MICHELE MORANO, author of *Grammar Lessons* and *Like Love*

"Robin Hemley interrogates the tangled histories, both private and public, that constitute his legacy as a writer, son, father, teacher, and citizen. *How to Change History*, a memoir in essays, features unforgettable characters from his extended family—his parents, both of whom were writers, an uncle who appeared on the *Dick Van Dyke Show*, an aunt-in-law who is believed to have cast evil spells on her family—as well as writers and artists he knew through their work and a stranger whose scrapbook he purchased at an estate sale. So much of every person's life is forgotten or never noticed in the first place. Against those odds Hemley achieves what he admires in *Death in the Woods* by Sherwood Anderson, which he identifies as 'a story about the observer trying to understand what it's like to be another person, an impossible necessity.' *How to Change History* delves into the past and delivers revelations that will always remain mysterious, as they must."
—KYOKO MORI, author of *Cat and Bird: A Memoir*

"In this rich and layered collection, Robin Hemley takes us on a fascinating tour of ruins, memories, scrapbooks, memorials, and mementos, luring the reader down each rabbit hole with a winning mixture of humor and vulnerability. At the same time, he is at work on a much larger theme in sketching a portrait of humanity through what we leave behind and how we try to stay the passage of time."
—SONYA HUBER, author of *Love and Industry: A Midwestern Workbook*

"Reading *How to Change History* is akin to sitting with an intimate friend, going through old photos and scrapbooks, conversing deep into the night about what connects us to the past and what might endure into the future. 'Everything is about letting go,' Robin Hemley writes, 'but still we let go reluctantly.' With his characteristic wit and keen acumen, Hemley inspects places near and far, even the most mundane sites—such as waiting rooms and flooded basements—for the wisdom they might offer us as we move through this temporary world."

—BRENDA MILLER, author of *A Braided Heart: Essays on Writing and Form*

"I wish Robin Hemley had written our actual history. In *How to Change History*, we are invited into a world where our uncle works on set with Dick Van Dyke, where our parents were not only writers but also knew all the cool writers and actors, including Larry, Curly, Shemp, and Moe, as well as William Carlos Williams. Where Provincetown is a kind of hometown and the Philippines is our backyard. Where true love is attending an Air Supply concert at the behest of true love. Not everything is perfect in this world, but if Hemley had devised our world, our lives would have been funnier, kinder, smarter, and more beautifully written. So, while our actual history was often painful, at least we have this book we can live in for a little while."

—NICOLE WALKER, author of *Processed Meats: Essays on Food, Flesh, and Navigating Disaster*

"Without saying as much, *How to Change History* works as a highly unselfconscious form of memoir, an intimate form of engagement with Robin Hemley's past but by way of broader subjects, which, as a methodology, has the effect of opening up the genre, the subjects at large, and the writer's life. In other words, this is an entirely fresh way of approaching memoir—and, to my mind, one that is far more engaging and, by way of storytelling, engages the reader in a shared exercise. This is a beautiful collection and pushes both the essay and memoir in new and necessary directions."

—LIA PURPURA, author of *All the Fierce Tethers*

"As a brilliant chronicler of both time and space, Robin Hemley's incursions into the past are about awareness: sometimes in the moment, sometimes years afterward. The past is its own country, and, unlike geographical countries, it shifts unexpectedly, so we never know when we might again, unaware, cross its border—as Hemley so insightfully does. As readers, we feel great sorrow and tenderness for the foreigners trapped in that ephemeral kingdom, because those foreigners are us."
—SUE WILLIAM SILVERMAN, author of *Acetylene Torch Songs: Writing True Stories to Ignite the Soul*

"The thing about Robin Hemley is the thing about all great essayists: subject matter is secondary; the writer is the draw. Let Hemley ponder whatever his attention wanders to—diaries or plaques or photographs or family misadventures or so much more, all of it with a pinch of complicating 'truth'—and I'm here for it, eagerly reading at snail's pace to savor every word, because it's oddball commentary that grants insight, not drama and suspense, and Hemley's mind is the consummate guide to this wonderful world we share."
—PATRICK MADDEN, author of *Disparates* and *Sublime Physick*

HOW TO CHANGE HISTORY

A Salvage Project

Robin Hemley

Acknowledgments for the use of copyrighted material appear on pages xiii–xiv, which constitute an extension of the copyright page.

The University of Nebraska Press is part of a land-grant institution with campuses and programs on the past, present, and future homelands of the Pawnee, Ponca, Otoe-Missouria, Omaha, Dakota, Lakota, Kaw, Cheyenne, and Arapaho Peoples, as well as those of the relocated Ho-Chunk, Sac and Fox, and Iowa Peoples.

Library of Congress Cataloging-in-Publication Data
Names: Hemley, Robin, 1958– author.
Title: How to change history: a salvage project / Robin Hemley.
Description: Lincoln: University of Nebraska Press, 2025.
Identifiers: LCCN 2024038708 (print) | LCCN 2024038709 (ebook)
ISBN 9781496240323 (trade paperback)
ISBN 9781496243089 (epub)
ISBN 9781496243096 (pdf)
Subjects: LCSH: Hemley, Robin, 1958– | Authors, American—20th century—Biography.
Classification: LCC PS3558.E47915 Z46 2025 (print) | LCC PS3558.E47915 (ebook) |
DDC 813/.54 [B]—dc23/eng/20241023
LC record available at https://lccn.loc.gov/2024038708
LC ebook record available at https://lccn.loc.gov/2024038709

Set in Arno Pro by A. Shahan.

For my friends and family in the Philippines
especially the brilliant and effervescent Burgos clan.

Here and Gone. That's what it is to be human,
I think. To be both someone and no one at once,
to hold a particular identity in the world (our
names, our places of origin, our family and
affectional ties) and to feel that solid set of ties
also capable of dissolution, slipping away, as we
become moments of attention.

—Mark Doty, *Still Life with Oysters and Lemon*

A piece of the body torn out by the roots might
be more to the point.

—James Agee, *Let Us Now Praise Famous Men*

Contents

Illustrations

Acknowledgments

Grateful acknowledgment is made to the following publications which originally published these essays:

After Montaigne: Contemporary Essayists Cover the Essays, eds. David
    Lazar and Patrick Madden: "Of the Affection of Fathers for Their
    Children"

Best Travel Writing: "For the Spirits of Guinaang"

Boulevard: "A Word from Our Sponsors," as "The Moment Juste"

Columbia: "In the Storeroom of Figments," as "The Storeroom of
    Playboy Males"

Conjunctions: "In the Theater of Half-Truths," as "A Simple Metaphysics"

Defunct: "In the Basement of Afflictions," as "Queen for a Day"

Essay Daily: "Skinny Dipping with James Agee," as "Majestic Ruins:
    The Work of James Agee"

*The Far Edges of the Fourth Genre: An Anthology of Explorations in
    Creative Nonfiction*, eds. Sean Prentiss and Joe Wilkins: "The
    Incomplete History of Mary Hilliard," as "Lines that Create Motion"

Flash Nonfiction Funny: 71 Very Humorous, Very True, Very Short Stories,
    eds. Tom Hazuka and Dinty W. Moore: "The Dachshund Endures"

Fourth Genre: "Jim's Corner"; "Reading History to My Mother"

Lapham's Quarterly: "How to Remove a Curse," as "Removing My Curse"

Manoa: "How to Change History," as "Roy Underwater"

McSweeney's Internet Tendency: "Feast for the Departed," as "All You
    Need Is Kevlar"; "How to Change History, Redux," as "The Longest

Day"; "The Hypocrite's Guide to Saving the Earth," as "Composting with the Rich"; "On the Island of Our Fathers' Ghosts," as "Old Ghosts of Corregidor"

New York Times: "A Reincarnation When I Didn't Want One," as "A Reincarnation and Just When I Didn't Need One"

Ninth Letter: "In the Storeroom of Petty Hatreds," as "No Pleasure but Meanness"

Ohioana Library Association Journal: "Something Must Be Understood," as "Something Has to Be Understood"

Overland: "In the Basement of Afflictions," as "Queen for a Day"

Paris Review Daily: "The Air Supply Guide to Matrimonial Bliss," as "Ululating to Air Supply"

Seattle Review: "For the Spirits of Guinaang"

Speculative Nonfiction: "The Unmentionable One," as "Of Curses and Beauty: The Memoirs of Mario Praz"

Tampa Review: "The Writer across the Table," as "Borges in Indiana"

In addition, I'm grateful to Laurie Sainburg for her generosity as well as my trusted friends and readers Xu Xi, Nicole Walker, Peter Parsons, Heidi Stalla, Will McDonald for his keen eye, and to Courtney Ochsner and my agent Malaga Baldi for their support.

I would also like to express my gratitude to the Rockefeller Foundation Bellagio Center, the Bogliasco Foundation, and Virginia Center for the Creative Arts.

HOW TO CHANGE HISTORY

Prologue

On a plane recently, I glanced a few seats over and spotted someone watching that iconic 1980s film *Wall Street*. What fascinated me was Daryl Hannah's hair, big blonde ringlets framing her face, her coiffure making me unable to see her as the twenty-something actor she was then. She looked to me like an impersonator, someone old wanting to hang on desperately to the styles of her youth. I suppose this is another way of saying the film looked dated, but it's more than that. What dogged me as I watched Daryl Hannah in growing horror (she might as well have been pulling out her dentures before she went to bed with Charlie Sheen) was that I had lived through that era too. What was I thinking? What was everyone thinking and why don't I still think that way? Not only was Daryl's Hannah's hair uncomical at the time, but it was the norm. And then a switch turned off, and just as suddenly, her hair looked stupid (and you must say the word "stupid" in your head with the kind of British bluntness and accent of, say, a Ricky Gervais).

Okay, nostalgia. There's that too. If I had my way entirely, I wouldn't invite nostalgia to the party at all, but I think we must let it in, though not allow it to stay too long or ply it with drinks because Nostalgia quickly goes weepy and limp and then you have a real mess on your hands and have to get an Uber.

What I'm interested in is this hypothetical light switch that makes something au courant one day and utterly stupid the next. Or at least irrelevant. Or forgotten entirely. People included.

I might have briefly worn a mullet. I definitely owned a Nehru shirt.

But perhaps I'm going about this a bit too glibly. Not everything defunct is laughable. That may be true of fashions and fads, but certain defunct technologies retain a trueness. I own two ancient phonographs, one an Edison player that spins blue wax cylinders, and a 78-speed phonograph from the 1920s that makes me neither nostalgic nor derisive. I just think it sounds great, scratches and all. I know that no one else cares for Annette Hanshaw singing "True Blue Lou" from 1929, but I do because of reasons that are so much a part of me I couldn't possibly verbalize them without reducing them to nothing. I love this song too as a surviving artifact from a distant past in which I was not alive. I am fascinated that Annette Hanshaw in her day was a star and people went around humming her songs and made love to her music and gained the courage to propose or break it all off or give it another shot, triggered by this music. And then they didn't.

Am I the only one (I don't think so) who, when watching *The Wizard of Oz* or listening to Annette Hanshaw, think—stupidly, I know—*What are they doing here? They're dead. That's not them but it is.* I can't look at Judy Garland without looking at her future too, the shambles of her alcohol- and drug-addicted life. I feel an odd concern and sympathy for the young woman in the film, knowing as I do that the studio will load her up with pills and that she will struggle for the rest of her life with addiction. The vital image of the sixteen-year-old on the screen seems almost a mockery, akin to the Wicked Witch mocking Dorothy when she sees Auntie Em in a magic globe. As Auntie Em frets over Dorothy's whereabouts, Dorothy tries to respond, but they are in different lands, on different plains. For me, watching this, Garland is as much a prisoner of her time as Dorothy is of the Wicked Witch. What I see most clearly in the magic globe is her defunctness. Here, I'm using the word "defunct" tragically, not comically, because the word is at least as tragic as it is comic. There is no escaping defunctness. We can only attempt to understand it and contemplate it and grope for the light switch. Think of this moment of attention as a light switch. Think of it as a toggle between defunctness and relevance. Think of these words as part reliquary, part rescue mission, part memorial.

PART 1

Indescribable People

In the Waiting Room of Dick Van Dyke

In my early twenties, my brother's father-in-law, a jovial man who seemed to be always smiling, stopped smiling for a moment and pointed to my bare shoulder. "You should get those checked by a doctor." By "those," he meant my moles and freckles, my "beauty marks" as my mother and grandmother had always called them. No one else in my family had them in such abundance, and no one paid them much attention. As a child, I'd been a devotee of the sun. My grandmother lived a block from the beach in Long Beach, New York, and I spent all my summers from seven in the morning until dusk playing in the sand and water, shirtless. I was a skinny kid, painfully skinny, and this is what my family worried about constantly, not my exposure to the sun. A photo of me, circa age nine, shows me lounging on a deck chair virtually naked except for my swim trunks. My uncle Bill is seated beside me, dressed in shorts, Izod shirt, and sneakers with socks pulled absurdly high. He's a large man, but not fat, a character actor known mostly for his roles in Three Stooges shorts. His stage name is Tiny Brauer and I am in awe of him.

My mother, behind the camera, takes our picture, but not because of his fame. She dismisses him as a "ham actor." To her, I am the famous one. I am Mom Famous. I am Pretzel Boy, my long legs curled beneath me. My skin is unblemished in the photo, but health as we know now is an illusion, and everything formerly innocent and attractive, like the sun, or freckles, might kill us.

The most memorable *Dick Van Dyke Show* episode on which my uncle Bill appeared was the one about the day Richie was born. Bill played the cab driver who was supposed to drive Laura to the hospital, but Rob, upon hearing that Laura is in labor, drives home and smashes into the waiting cab. That's when Bill enters the house and explains that the bumpers of the two cars are locked and that he can't move. "It's like they're fused together," he says of the bumpers in his Brooklyn accent, his hangdog face displaying not anger but simple resignation. He makes an accompanying hand gesture, locking his fingers together to show Rob and Laura exactly what he means.

In the world of Dick Van Dyke, there were never any consequences. He tripped over the ottoman in the opening sequence of the show, or he didn't (in later opening sequences), displaying not his clumsiness but his mastery of physical comedy, this tall, lanky man who, offstage, "was mostly drunk for fifteen years," and who, like me, was married to a woman named Margie. That he knew my great-uncle Bill, who appeared in several episodes of *The Dick Van Dyke Show*, was reason enough to idolize Bill.

In another (Bill-less) episode of *The Dick Van Dyke Show*, a friend of Rob's son Richie connects the dots on Rob's back as he's sleeping on the couch, and discovers that together they form an image of the Liberty Bell. Rob and Laura and Richie, intrigued by the configuration, don't think "Cancer!" but "Ripleys," or as it's referred to in the show, "Odd but True." Rob visits the show's studios where he meets oddballs whose personalities are stranger than their supposed rare and eccentric treasures.

Once my brother's father-in-law planted the idea in me, I felt certain that I was going to die—I had never been so certain before—but now I knew, yes, something is going to kill me and I thought I knew exactly what. A raised bump on the inside of my leg, slightly red and hard as a pebble. I could squeeze it underneath the skin, feel its shape, imagine taking a knife and cutting it out. But its roots—how far did they reach and were they even visible?

I was twenty-three when I finally had them checked. Around the same time, I began to have a recurring dream that I was in the waiting room of Dick Van Dyke's offices. I had to wait for Dick Van Dyke in the waiting room an awfully long time before he would see me.

What does it mean when a place is described as nondescript? Only a non-place would be nondescript or someone too lazy to describe a place might say it was nondescript. I don't think the word "lazy" describes me, but if ever there was a place that was nondescript, Dick Van Dyke's dream realm waiting room was it. If you want to get personal about it, I suppose I could be nondescribed too, as a nondescript looking white guy of nondescript height, and nondescriptly overweight. This waiting room was the waiting room equivalent of me.

As I waited for Mr. Van Dyke, I felt certain he would at least remember my uncle Bill who, in my mind at least, was the epitome of descript. After all, I had been granted this audience, hadn't I? So he must have remembered my uncle Bill fondly. Together we would laugh about the handful of episodes he had appeared in. "It's like they're fused together," Mr. Van Dyke would say, imitating Bill's hangdog look. "Brilliant!" And I would bask in the sunlight of Dick Van Dyke's appreciation and attention.

In the waiting room of my doctor's office, I imagined all the ways I might be erased before my time. I held many funerals for myself in that waiting room. One moment I was full of self-pity. The next I was the admirable stoic. I felt thoroughly Shakespearean, not a ham actor at all, in my waiting room gloom, all the mind a stage. You would not have known this from my outward demeanor, which was ridiculously cheerful, even obsequious around my doctor, as though I needed to convince her not to let me die. My doctor was a medical intern in her early thirties. She traded one fear for another. The mole that worried me so was not really a mole after all and was completely harmless. To this day, it sits on the inner portion of my leg, no bigger than it was when I was twenty-three, a reminder to me that my idea of my body and the fact of it are two different things.

Other moles concerned my doctor. These were dark, irregularly shaped, growing. *Beauty mark* and *freckle* were words displaced by others in my early twenties. I learned new phrases: *dysplastic nevi syndrome* and *pre-cancerous*. Mr. Mole, my doctor called me. Over a hundred dotted my back, and they were arranged in a "classic configuration" for a male. Not like the Liberty Bell, unfortunately. Women most often have them on their legs. Men have them on their backs. I had more than my doctor had ever seen, and this excited her. This was, after all, a teaching hospital, and my back was a Teachable Back. Photos were taken, students led in to take a look at my classic configuration.

The excisions began. First, the poke of the needle, so long and thin like a giant mosquito's probe. But it felt more like the sting of a yellow jacket, prolonged, the way it felt when at the age of seven I ran into a hive of yellow jackets and received over a hundred stings. How prescient those yellow jackets were.

Count to five as exquisite hairs of pain fizzle and fry. One Mississippi. Two Mississippi. From hair to glass to shards breaking over my back. The mole is me, for a moment, all of me, as I'm reduced to one tiny field, recipient of the liquid hive.

She pokes under my skin, withdraws, takes the needle, and places it again a mere centimeter from the last place she stung me. Again. Sometimes as many as five times depending on the size of the mole and the area to be numbed. She cuts them out or burns them off. Classic configuration for her, but terror for Mr. Mole. I smell the smoke of my burning flesh, hear the electric crackle like a bug zapper. Local anesthetic does not dull the sound of my singed skin or the scrape, the gristle. There is nothing like the sounds of unfeeling as you sense that cutting away, that tugging. Yes, that's what it is, a tugging. Sometimes she uses what she calls cookie cutters.

"I think we got it all," she says.

And "Tell me if it hurts, if you feel anything."

And "The blood, there, yes, stanch it."

And waiting for the results. "We'll let you know if we find anything."

My dream repeated for many years, as did my moles. Every year, I'd wait in the waiting room for Dick Van Dyke, hoping to meet him. Every year I'd have my moles excised until the doctors told me that the new thinking about moles was not to remove them, but just to watch and wait for any change. All that pain for nothing, as it turns out. Almost none of the excised moles, when examined in a lab, were anything unusual. They were mostly in the end, run-of-the-mill, nondescript moles. Only the waiting room mattered, all those photos on the wall of memorable scenes.

A receptionist told me to make myself comfortable while waiting for Mr. Van Dyke, who was running a little behind schedule. The room's decor was neutral, its furniture functional, magazines on the tables. I don't know why

Dick Van Dyke bothered to see me—it was a kind of courtesy call. The reality, of course, was that my uncle was a bit player whom Dick Van Dyke would probably never have remembered. I was a nobody too, less than Bill, one of the millions of nameless people who flock the earth like birds and disappear without even saying one line recorded for posterity.

While I waited for Dick Van Dyke and rehearsed what I was going to say to him, I searched the various pictures for episodes in which I might have appeared, though I knew that I had appeared in none. I searched and waited. I must have dreamed of the waiting room a dozen times over the years, and each time, I felt both fortunate to be there and slightly unsettled that my meetings kept being postponed. I haven't had that dream for at least fifteen years. In the final dream, I wanted to leave but was afraid I'd miss my chance if I did, though it was apparent that the office was now closed and the receptionist had left for the day, and the lights were off. I guess that on some level I must have finally understood that I wasn't waiting for Dick Van Dyke at all. The waiting room was its own destination, the wait itself the entire point.

Somewhere in some textbook my back is famous. But maybe even I wouldn't be able to tell it was my back anymore. It's a young back, perhaps not as slouched by life as it is now, and quite literally of course, every molecule of that back has been replaced. When med students look at my back and try to pick out which moles look dangerous and which benign, do they wonder who belongs to that back? Do they wonder how long I lived? Do they wonder if the moles multiplied, if they became something that made sense, like the Liberty Bell? Or do they see them as merely a meaningless field of black dots on a scarred landscape, fused together? Do they wonder if I waited too long?

Reading History to My Mother

Your silence will not protect you.
—Audre Lorde

"Everything's mixed up in those boxes, the past and the present," my mother tells me. "Those movers made a mess of everything." I'm visiting her at the Leopold late on a Monday night after reading to my kids and being read to by my eldest, who at six is rightfully proud of her newfound reading ability. My mother and I have been readers for many years, but in some ways, she finds reading more difficult than my six-year-old. At eighty-two, my mother's eyesight has deteriorated. Glaucoma. Severe optic nerve damage to her left eye. Macular degeneration. Tomorrow, I'm taking her to the doctor for a second laser operation to "relieve the pressure." We have been told by the doctor that the surgery won't actually improve her eyesight, but, with luck, will stop it from deteriorating any more. After that there's another operation she'll probably undergo, eighty miles south in Seattle. Another operation that won't actually make her see any better.

"I always had such good eyesight," she tells me. And then, "I wish there was something that could improve my eyesight." And then, "When are we going to go shopping for that new computer?"

"Well, let's make sure you can see the screen first," I say, which sounds cruel, but she has complained to me tonight that she wasn't able to see any of the words on her screen, though I think this has less to do with her eyesight than the glasses she's wearing. Unnaturally thick and foggy. My mother looks foggy too, almost drunk, disheveled in her dirty sweater, though she doesn't drink. It's probably the medicine she's been taking for her many conditions. My mother owns at least half a dozen pairs of eyeglasses, and I know I should have sorted through them all by now (we tried once), but so many things have gone wrong in the last five months since my mother moved to Bellingham that sorting through her glasses is a side issue. I get up from the couch in the cramped living room of her apartment, step over the coffee table—careful not to tip over the cup of peppermint tea I'm drinking out of a beer stein, careful not to bump into my mother—and cross to the bedroom crammed with wardrobe boxes and too much furniture, though much less than what she's used to. On her dresser there are parts of various eyeglasses: maimed glasses, the corpses of eyeglasses, a dark orphaned lens here, a frame there, an empty case, and one case with a pair that's whole. This is the one I grab and take to my mother who is waiting patiently, always patient these days, or perhaps so unnerved and exhausted that it passes for patience. She takes the case from me and removes the old glasses, places them beside her beer mug of licorice tea, and puts on the new pair.

She rubs an eye, says, "This seems to be helping. Maybe these are my reading glasses." I should know, of course. I should have had them color-coded by now, but I haven't yet.

She bends down to the photo from the newsletter on the coffee table, and says, "Yes, that's William Carlos Williams."

A little earlier she told me about the photo. "It's in one of those boxes," she told me. "I saw it the other day. I thought I'd told you about it before," but she hadn't, this photo of her with William Carlos Williams, Theodore Roethke, and other famous writers. So I spent fifteen minutes rifling through her boxes of bills and old papers mixed up on the kitchen counter (a Cascade Gas Company bill, final payment requested for service at the apartment she moved into in December, when we still thought she could live on her own; a letter from the superintendent of public schools of New York City, dated 1959, addressed to my grandmother, a teacher at the time, telling her how many sick days she was allowed), looking for the photo, until she explained that it was actually part of a newsletter from the artists' colony Yaddo, in Saratoga Springs, New York. Armed with that crucial bit of information, I found it.

The photo is captioned "Class picture, 1950."

Not many of these people are smiling. Eugenie Gershoy, seated next to Jessamyn West, has a little smirk, and Mitsu Yashima, seated next to Flossie Williams, smiles broadly, and also Cid Corman in the back row, whom I met when I was a high school exchange student in Japan. My mother visited me in Osaka and we traveled by train to Kyoto, to Cid Corman's ice cream parlor where I ate a hamburger, had an ice cream cone, and listened to a poetry reading while my mother and Cid reminisced.

"Don't I look prim?" my mother says, and she does. Or maybe it's something else. Scared? Intimidated? Shocked? My mother was thirty-four then— This was a year or so before she met my father. My sister, Nola, was three, and my mother was an up-and-coming young writer, one novel published. John Crowe Ransom liked her work and published several of her stories in the *Kenyon Review*.

She stands up straight, hands behind her back, a scarf tied loosely around her neck, draping down over a breast, a flower pinned to the scarf. Theodore Roethke stands, huge, imposing, dour. In an accompanying article, Harvey Shapiro tells of how publicly Roethke liked to display his wounds, how he told Shapiro of his hurt that John Crowe Ransom had rejected "My Papa's Waltz," though Roethke was famous by then and the poem had been widely anthologized. What remained, still, was Roethke's pain, perhaps the pain of rejection meshed with the pain of the poem's subject matter—abuse at the hands of his drunken father. Shapiro also tells of Roethke's claim that he'd bummed his way to Yaddo after escaping "in drag" from a mental institution on the West Coast earlier that summer. "He liked to romanticize his mental illness," Shapiro writes. Perhaps, but something honest still comes across in that picture, the despair clear for anyone to view head-on.

In the front row, William Carlos Williams sits cross-legged, dignified.

"He dreamed of my legs," my mother tells me.

"William Carlos Williams dreamed of your legs?" I ask.

"At breakfast one day he said he'd had a dream about my legs. 'That girl has nice legs,' he said."

We have to keep going back over histories, our own and the histories of others, constantly revising. There's no single truth . . . except that, perhaps. History is not always recorded and not always written by the victor. History is

Fig. 1. "Class Photo," Yaddo, 1950. From left, top: William Osborne, Theodore Roethke, Robel Paris, Harvey Shapiro, Elaine Gottlieb, Beryl Levy, Cid Corman, Simmons Persons, Gladys Farnel, Hans Sahl, Clifford Wright, Richard Eberhart. From left, bottom: Ben Weber, Nicholas Callas, Jessamyn West, Eugenie Gershoy, William Carlos Williams, Flossie Williams, Mitsu Yashima, Charles Schucker, Elizabeth Ames, John Dillon Husband. Used by permission of the Yaddo Corporation.

not always written. We carry our secret histories behind our words, in another room, in the eyeglass case on the dresser in the bedroom. Maybe someone comes along and finds the right pair. Maybe we have too many, unsorted.

My mother's former landlord, Loyce, wants to know the history of the "L." I was gone for the past week in Hawaii, and that's the only reason I haven't called before now. Loyce has left messages for me twice, ostensibly to see about getting back my mother's deposit to us; minus a charge for mowing, the ad for renting the apartment again, a reasonable charge for her time, and of course, for painting over the L. She'd also like the keys back from us. But the L is the real reason she's called. My mother wrote an "L" on the wall of the apartment in indelible magic marker before she left. "I'm dying to know the story," Loyce says. "I know there's a good story behind it."

Loyce appreciates a good story, and this is one of the things I appreciate about Loyce, that and her compassion. She moved to Bellingham several years ago to take care of her ailing mother, and now lives in her mother's old house on top of a hill with a view of the bay and the San Juan Islands. So she understands our situation. She knows that my mother can't live alone anymore, that all of us were taken by surprise at the condition she was in when she moved here five months ago. Until then, my mother had been living on her own in South Bend, Indiana, where she taught writing until ten years ago. She'd been living on her own since I moved out at the age of sixteen to go to boarding school and had been taking care of herself for the past thirty years since my father's death. But in the last several months, things have fallen apart. Our first inkling was the mover, a man in his sixties who worked with his son. He took me aside on the first day and told me that in his thirty years of moving he'd never seen an apartment as messy as my mother's. When he and his son went to my mom's apartment in South Bend, they almost turned around.

"You don't have to do this if you don't want," the mover told his son.

No, the first inkling was my brother's call from LA, where my mother was visiting a few days prior to her big move. The van had loaded in South Bend and she'd flown to LA to visit him and his family. The night before her flight from LA to Seattle, he called me near midnight and said, "Mom's hallucinating."

I asked him what he meant, what she was seeing, and he told me that she was seeing all these people who didn't exist and making strange remarks. "When I picked her up at the airport, she said there was a group of Asians having a baby. She said they were a troupe of actors, and they were doing a skit."

Still, the next day, he put her on the plane to Seattle, and I picked her up and brought her to her new home. Since then, we have gone to three different doctors and my mother has had brain scans and blood tests and sonograms of her carotid arteries and been placed on a small dose of an antipsychotic drug. One doctor says her cerebral cortex has shrunk, and she's had a series of tiny strokes to individual arteries in her brain.

At 3:00 a.m. one morning, the police call me and say that my mother thinks someone is trying to break into her apartment.

"Is there anyone living with her?" the policeman asks.

"No."

"She says a handicapped woman lives with her. You might want to see a doctor about this."

I take her to doctors and try to convince my mother that she needs to live where she can be safe, but she refuses to even consider it. "I should have stayed in New York," she tells me. "I never should have left." And then, "I should never have come here. Why can't you be on my side?" And then, "I'll move down to LA. Your brother is much nicer than you are."

I spend a few nights at her apartment, and she tells me about the Middle Eastern couple who have taken over her bedroom and the children who are there, and the landlord comes over and puts a lock on the door from the kitchen to the garage, though we know no one was trying to break in. And homeless people are living on her back porch. And she keeps startling people in the garage who are removing her belongings.

But finally.

After my cousin David flies up from LA. After visiting a dozen managed care facilities, after my brother says he thinks it's the medicine that's doing this and I talk to the doctors and the doctors talk to each other and they talk to my mother and she says, "The doctor says I'm fine," and I say "No, he doesn't," and she hangs up, turns off her hearing aid.

Coincidentally, a friend of my mother in South Bend wins second place in a poetry competition run by the literary journal I edit. The poems were all anonymous, and I had nothing to do with the judging, but my mother's friend has won second prize for a poem about her delusional mother, called "My Mother and Dan Rather." I call her up to tell her the good news of her award, but she assumes, of course, I'm calling to talk about my mother. So that's what we do for half an hour. She tells me she's distanced herself over the last year from my mother because she seemed too much like her own mother, and she tells me that several of my mother's friends wondered if they should call me and let me know what was going on.

I almost forget to tell her about her prize.

No, the first inkling was two years ago. My wife wondered aloud about my mother's memory, her hold on reality. I told her my mother had always been kind of scattered, messy, unfocused.

And finally. After I come into her apartment one day and feel the heat, I go to the stove and turn off the glowing burners. My mother has a blister on her hand the size of a walnut. My wife tells me that it's ridiculous for my mother to live alone, that somehow we have to force her to move. "What if she sets the apartment on fire? She might not only kill herself but the people next door."

"I know," I tell her. "I'm trying," but I also know that short of a court order, short of being declared her legal guardian, I can't force her.

And finally. I convince my mother to come with me to the Leopold, a historic hotel in downtown Bellingham that has been converted into apartments for seniors, one wing assisted living, the other independent. We have lunch there one day. My mother likes the food.

And finally she agrees to spend a couple of weeks there in a guest room.

Famous people stayed at the Leopold, I tell my mother. Rutherford B. Hayes. Jenny Lind, the Swedish Nightingale. This doesn't impress her. She has known more famous people than can fit on a plaque. But she has a nice view of the bay, somewhat blocked by the Georgia Pacific Paper Mill. And she likes the food, but the apartment is only two cramped rooms, and across the street at the Greek restaurant, people party until 2:00 a.m. each night and climb trees and conduct military rituals. And the Iraqi army rolled through the streets one night. And a truck dumped two bodies, a man and a woman dressed in formal evening attire.

"They sometimes flood the parking lot," she tells me. "And use it as a waterway."

Or, "Look at that," pointing, reaching for nothing.

She keeps returning to the apartment, driven by the woman I've hired to clean it. My mother wants to drive again, and I tell her no, she can't possibly, and I read articles and watch programs that tell me not to reverse roles, not to become the parent, and I wonder how that's possible to avoid. One day, I walk into her apartment and find signs she's posted all around on the bed, in the guest room, on the kitchen counter. "Keep Off." "Stay Out." "Go Away." I ask her about these signs, and she tells me they're just a joke. She's become wary of me. I tell her she's safe, ask her why she feels so threatened. She tells me, "I've never felt safe in my life."

During this period, my mother writes her "L" on the wall of the kitchen.

And the weeks at the Leopold have turned to months, and now most of her belongings are stuffed into a heated mini-storage unit. More of her belongings are stuffed into the basement of the Leopold.

Finally.

I almost don't want to tell Loyce the story of the L when she calls. I'd like to keep her in suspense, because sometimes that's stronger than the truth. She probably thinks it's about her, that the "L" stands for Loyce, but it doesn't. It stands for Leopold. One day my mother was at the apartment, after we finally convinced her that she had to move, and I gave her a magic marker and asked her to mark the boxes she'd like taken to the Leopold. Apparently, she thought she was marking a box, but she was really marking the wall. This is what she really wanted. That was not lost on me. She loved that apartment. She wanted her independence, but this was just too much for me to move.

Loyce and I say goodbye after I assure her that I'll return the keys and she assures me she'll return most of the deposit. It's already eight thirty and I told my mother I'd be over around eight, but I had to read to my kids first. I haven't seen them in a week. I've just returned from Hawaii.

In Hawaii, where I've been researching a new book, I had more fun than I probably should have. Not the kind of fun with life-bending consequences, but fun nonetheless, hanging out with a former student, eating out every night, smoking cigars, drinking. For ten dollars a day more, I was told at the airport, I could rent a convertible—a Ford Mustang, or a Caddie, and I'm not ready for that, so I take the Mustang. Stupid. The wife of the friend I'm staying with laughed when she saw it in her driveway. "Oh," she tells me. "I thought maybe Robbie was having a mid-life crisis." No, it's me probably, even though I hate to admit it. I refuse to believe such a thing could happen to me at this preordained age, a month from forty, that I could be saddled with such a cliché crisis, such mediocre regrets.

My daughter wants to read to me tonight, all seven stories from an Arnold Lobel book. "They're short," she assures me. We compromise on three, her three favorites. One of these she read last week to her class while I was in Hawaii. My wife, who sometimes works in our daughter's class as a volunteer, has already told me that the class was enthralled. "She acted so confident. She took her time and showed them the pictures."

The one she read to her class, "The Journey," is about a mouse who wants to visit his mother, and in a sequence of transactions, acquires a car, roller skates, boots, sneakers, and finally a new set of feet. When he reaches his mother she hugs him, kisses him, and says, "Hello, my son, you are looking fine—and what nice new feet you have!" The whole class broke out in hysterical laughter, my daughter assured me.

I've brought my mother a box of chocolate-covered macadamia nuts. She looks at it, bewildered. "Oh, I thought it was a book," she says.

I make tea for us, but she only has a few tea mugs and they're dirty, so we have to use beer steins. "I've ended up with such an odd assortment of things," she tells me, and she blames this on the movers.

A week before my trip to Hawaii, I visited her and she showed me a notebook in which she'd kept a journal during the midseventies. My mother has kept journals from the time she was sixteen, a series of secret histories written in any notebook she can find. But now, she cannot read these histories, and she asks me to read this one to her.

"I might use it in a story," she tells me. "It's about Moe and Helen." Moe is Moe Howard of the Three Stooges. He was a cousin of ours by marriage, and whenever she visited California, she'd stop by to see them. Moe, who had such a violent on-screen persona: Think of him saying, "Wise guy, eh?" Poking the eyes of Larry, Curly, Shemp, or one of the later pseudo-Stooges, Curly Joe and Joe Besser. I met him once, a frail old man with white hair, too quiet to seem like Moe. Off-screen, he was a gentle family man, kind and grateful to his fans, never refusing to sign an autograph. What my mother wants me to read to her is an account of the last time she saw Moe and his wife, Helen, when they were both dying.

Seeing Moe and Helen was touching—a beautiful hill of purple flowers outside that Moe said was all theirs—a beautifully furnished, expensively comfortable house through which they glide, ghost-like. They don't kiss me because of the possibility of germs. Helen is in a loose purple nylon dressing gown. She has been recuperating from a breast operation and says in a slightly quaking voice that she will be going to the doctor soon and will probably have cobalt.

Moe is red-faced and very thin. His thinness, wispiness, makes him look elfin—because he used to be heavier, he seemed bigger. His hair is white. He smiles proudly, talking about his appearances at colleges and his memoirs which comprise many books. Talk about the film I am supposed to have made with him. He reminds me that I acted in it (at the age of about 19) 8mm, I think, with his children. But it is packed somewhere with thousands of feet of other film.

As I'm reading this to my mother, I feel odd, wondering if she notices the similarities between this passage and her own present life—the things packed away, the memories, the frailty—but I say nothing about this, though it moves me. Instead, I ask her about this film she was in, and she tells me it was an impromptu home movie in which Moe was cast as the villain, of course, and she was the protector of his children. She has never seen it, but it exists somewhere. Moe's daughter, Joan, once showed me the huge roll of home movies in her attic. Toward the end of his life, Moe took every home movie he made and spliced them all together onto one monstrous cumbersome roll that no one could ever possibly watch in its entirety. Somewhere on this roll exists a movie with my mother, age nineteen, circa 1935. Silently, I flip through other pages in my mother's journal, as she sits near me, lost in her memories, needing no journal really.

I am not in fantasy land. I am painfully living out my loneliness and nostalgia. I dream of my son every night and wish he were here. Those who have died are intolerably absent and I feel that all the love I need and want will not come because I had my chance and lost it, and what man will be responsible for or will react to my aging, my passion, my intolerable loneliness . . . ?

I am with her now, but not. We see each other through veils. We have battled for this moment, and neither sees the other as we would like.

William Carlos Williams dreamed of my mother's legs, as did other men that summer of 1950 at Yaddo.

As we bend over the class photo, circa 1950, she tells me the official history of that summer, how special it was for her, how it was so exciting to be around such vital intellects, such talented writers. "It was really something, going down to breakfast and having conversations with all these people. The talent was never quite the same after that."

I tell her I'd love to have a copy of this picture. "You could write to Yaddo," she says. "They use it for publicity." She tells me I could write to the poet Harvey Shapiro, who is pictured with her. "It's the least he could do," she says, with what seems like bitterness, and I let this remark wash over me because I think I know what's behind it.

Once, a number of years ago, my wife and my mother and I were on a drive, and I was telling her about a friend of mine who'd done his dissertation on the poetry of Shapiro. From the back seat my mother blurted, "You know, he raped me."

My wife and I looked at one another. We didn't say anything. We didn't know what to say. The remark was so sudden, so unexpected, we hardly knew how to react. We were silent, all three of us. Neither my wife nor I mentioned this to each other later.

My mother starts talking about him now, though I haven't asked. She says, "One time, he invited me to a private party, and innocent that I was, I went there." In memory, she's lucid. Only the present is slippery, tricky, untrustworthy.

"There were all these men there. They were all leches. Ted Roethke kept lunging for me, just making grabs. He really had problems," and she laughs. She mentions Shapiro, whom she trusted. He was younger than her, than all these other famous men. "I thought he'd protect me." She laughs again. This time, there's no mistaking the bitterness.

I think about asking her. What term to use? "He assaulted you?"

"Yes," she says.

"Did it happen at Yaddo?" I ask.

She nods.

"Did you ever confront him?"

"No," she says. "I don't want to talk about it."

But then she says, "There wasn't much I could do. In those days, there wasn't much to do. I just pretended it didn't happen. For a little while, he became my boyfriend."

I don't know what to say. I probably shouldn't say anything. I sigh. "He should have been locked up. How could he be your boyfriend after that?"

"He was drunk when it happened," and I want to say that's no excuse, but I keep my mouth shut and let her talk. "I left the party early and he followed me back to my room. I tried to lock the door, but the lock was broken.

"I turned things around. I had to. I was confused. In my mind, he became my protector from the other men there."

I study the picture again. My mother's expression and the expressions of the men. I wonder when this photo was taken, before or after the assault my mother describes. The photo has taken on the quality of a group mug shot to me. I think they look like jerks, most of them—except for Cid Corman, whom my mother says is a wonderful person, and maybe some others, too, maybe William Carlos Williams, who dreamed of my mother's legs and "had an eye for the ladies" as my mother says. Maybe even dour Theodore Roethke, though he lunged at her as though she was something being wheeled by on a dessert tray.

"They weren't famous for their personalities," she tells me.

I think about these people in the photo, how unfair it seems to me that someone can go on to have a career, hide behind his smirk, have dissertations written about him, how the actions of some people seem to have no visible consequences. I think of my mother's secret histories, her journals, her blurted comments, her assertion that she has never felt safe.

I flip the newsletter over to the section titled "Recent Works Produced by Yaddo Fellows," and see that the latest works reported are from 1987. For an absurd moment, I believe that none of the Fellows at Yaddo have been productive for many years, and this makes me happy, but then I realize the newsletter itself is very old.

My mother has taken to carrying a picture of me. Ideal Me, I call it, skinny, sitting languorously, smiling beside a life-size cardboard cut-out of Rudolph Valentino. The son she longed for in her journal perhaps hardly exists any-more—I was away at boarding school that year, my choice, not hers, and I never returned.

I have come to visit her now. I've knocked lightly. I've used my key. She can barely see me when I walk into her apartment. I've told her I've returned from Hawaii, that she can expect me around eight, but I'm late and as I push open the door, she's looking at me almost suspiciously, because really her eyesight is that bad, and until I speak she has no idea who's entering. The Iraqi army? A stranger who wants her belongings? A poet she thinks is her "protector" but means her harm? I half expect to see signs, "Keep Off," "Stay Out," "Go Away." I have brought a box of chocolate-covered macadamia nuts. I am wearing new feet, but she doesn't notice. Tomorrow she will have sur-gery on her eyes that will not improve anything but keep things from getting worse. How much worse could things get for this woman who loves words, but can neither see nor write them anymore? Does her history go on inside her, on some gigantic roll of spliced-together home movies? Tell me the story of the L. Tell me the story of the wall of your apartment. Tell me the story of those talented writers who publicly display their wounds and the writers who secretly wound others. Tell me which is worse. She kisses me lightly and I give her her gift. And she says, once, only once, though I keep hearing it, the disappointment, and strangely, even fear, "Oh, I thought it was a book."

The Incomplete History of Mary Hilliard

All memory is individual, unreproducible—it dies with each person.
  —Susan Sontag, *Regarding the Pain of Others*

"All memory is individual, unreproducible." But a scrapbook is a quote from memory, much as a snapshot is a quote. When the person dies to whom that scrapbook belonged, the scrapbook alchemizes over time into an artifact without context, rising out of the anonymous pile in a junk store or at an estate sale. This is how I came to own the scrapbook of Mary Wilson Hilliard, born May 28, 1919, in Easton, Pennsylvania. I found it at an estate sale one Saturday morning while I was in residence at the Virginia Center for the Creative Arts. Several of the other fellows at VCCA and I decided to take a break from our individual projects and search for barbecue and garage sales. My memory of this day has mostly faded. I'm in the backseat of someone else's car and I'm not even sure who is seated with me. Helen B? I don't think Helen would go in for either barbecue or garage sales. Lisa Z? The same. Lisa S? Yes, almost surely. And surely this outing was at my instigation because that's what I do. I instigate.

We can't remember our lives day by day, and even if we could, even if we photographed our days at ten-minute intervals, what would this mean at the end of a life? A number of diarists have recorded the minutiae of their days, even down to their bowel movements. The desire to memorialize life is almost as hopeless as the desire to live forever. Thomas Mallon writes in *A Book of One's Own: People and Their Diaries* that there is always an intended audience for a diary—sometimes posterity, sometimes grandchildren, sometimes a future self. Undoubtedly, the same is true of scrapbooks, but instead of the minutiae of a day or the feelings or observations of that day, the scrapbook hits only the highs, not the lows, of a life. With only a caption or two, there's not much to go on, so where's the interest to anyone else? But it does interest me, or at least this scrapbook interested me when I found it on a table in the basement of a church along a sun-drenched Virginia road one August morning on an otherwise unremarkable day of my life.

The book has a heavy leather cover of reddish brown, and it bulges with perhaps a hundred construction paper pages on which are glued the ephemera of Mary Wilson Hilliard's life. I have never seen a scrapbook like it. It covers only six years of her life, from 1940 to 1946, and I was told by one of the people holding the sale (a professional outfit with no relation to Mary Hilliard) that a companion scrapbook also existed, from the 1930s, but someone had already purchased it, and there was no record of who that was. Why that person didn't purchase this scrapbook as well is obvious to me. The price was not cheap. The cost of the remaining scrapbook was seventy-five dollars, and who would buy someone else's scrapbook for such an outrageous price?

Rhetorical question.

I understand why it was so expensive. Every page is crammed with letters, engagement announcements, the stockings she wore throughout World War II, a newspaper proclaiming the invasion of Normandy, a woven bracelet made by one of her traumatized army patients when she worked as a volunteer at Walter Reed Hospital in Washington, DC. There are playbills from dramas and musicals she saw, a beautifully preserved menu from Antoine's restaurant in New Orleans, circa 1943: A bowl of gumbo sets you back thirty-five cents. Her birth certificate. A Hawaiian lei from a cruise she took. Her Red Cross pin. A balloon from the Shriners' Circus. The button from a military uniform. Election paraphernalia from the first election in which she voted. Her voter registration card. She voted for Wendell Willkie against Roosevelt. She was a Republican, at least in 1940, and she attended a rally for Willkie on October 4, 1940. A little song sheet printed on both sides sits loose in the scrapbook, as do many of the artifacts—some that have come unglued, some that undoubtedly she simply pressed between the pages of the book.

SING FOR WILLKIE

Vital Campaign Messages, set to tunes everyone knows and enjoys. *Everybody Sing! and Win with Willkie!*

My money is all spent for taxes—My money I don't even see; It all goes to Washington Bureaus O bring back my money to me.
Chorus: Bring back, bring back—O bring back my money to me, to me; Bring back, bring back. O bring back my money to me.

Mary and I don't have much in common politically, but we share the same birthday.

And there are mysteries embedded in the scrapbook. There's Robert, the bomber pilot she dated. Several photos show him posed by his bomber with his crew, some photos show him with Mary. And there's this telegram Robert sent her on December 29, 1945:

Willie: I'll be in Washington for New Year's Eve. Would like to see you very much. I'll call you Sunday morning. Love, Robert.

And there are captions. The most intriguing, referred to twice on the same page:

"Before tar baby arrived."
"After tar baby arrived."

The term comes from the Br'er Rabbit stories, a term not widely used these days as it's perceived as racist. But in Mary's day it would have referred to a sticky situation—sadly ironic in this case as the glue on which she pasted her photo or memento of tar baby didn't hold. Whatever was held there is held no longer. Perhaps if I look at the placement of the captions, I'll be able to piece together an explanation. The captions are in the section when she worked as a Red Cross volunteer at Walter Reed in March 1944. I know this because the preceding page has a photo of her with all the other volunteers, forty-three in all, behind which she tucked her supervisor's evaluation of her: "Miss Hilliard needs help in recognizing and understanding the underlying elements of human behavior, the implications of illness, and the role of a social worker in this setting, though in April she was considering attending social work school. She now has decided she does not want to do this." Mary worked on Ward 24, and she seems to have been fond of one patient in particular, whom she refers to simply as "Grande." She captions a couple of spots with the words, "Grande's handiwork, Ward 24," and one of these pieces has survived, a beautifully woven bracelet of black and white—I'm not sure of the material—that Grande must have given her.

It's likely that the buyer of Mary's other scrapbook butchered it to sell its ephemera, which surely is worth more separately than in its present bulky form.

The problems here are many. Do I want to reconstruct her life? Yes. I am fascinated by this person whom I never met and feel a strange urge to piece together who she was. But I'm interested as much in the artifact-ness of this scrapbook, the idea of private memorialization, the shrines we construct to tell us who we were and that we never consider will someday wind up sold to a complete stranger at an estate sale. I don't want either to sentimentalize her or to show her disrespect. I want to inventory these six years of her life and write about each defunct object in a way to revivify it, or at least to take this small museum and enlarge it, to consider it as an archaeologist might. A tomb. A dig. The tiny treasures of a life. I want to consider our small treasures, our milestones—these things that make up a life or part of it. In the scrapbook, I see a sliver of her mind at work, though I can't possibly know her in all her complexity, as I can't even know myself. But the scrapbook bobbed out of her consciousness into mine in a church basement in Virginia, and it seemed to suggest we shared an affinity besides our mutual day of birth. It seemed to suggest I buy it.

And so I did.

Jim's Corner

Ever since Jim died, whose last name I can't even remember, I have hated plaques. Not plaque as in the white stuff that clings to your teeth, but the commemorative kind. Memorial plaques are a lie, one of the many lies we have tacitly agreed upon as a society to make death less terrifying. Other comfortable lies include the endings of most Hollywood movies (no surprise there), if you work toward your dream it will come true (sometimes it doesn't and you have to settle for less), love conquers all, hope springs eternal, what goes around comes around, the bigger they come the harder they fall, everything happens for a reason, every ending is a new beginning. Nationwide is on your side. Like a good neighbor, State Farm is there. We'll always have Paris.

Plaques are evil because they leave the impression that the future cares. Get this: the future doesn't care.

An example: Jim, whose last name I have forgotten. He was an associate professor in the English Department in Charlotte, North Carolina, where I held my first job as an assistant professor when I was twenty-eight. A short, stocky guy with a friendly face, Jim stood out in the hall near the copying room smoking and collaring anyone who would listen. Now that seems like the Pleistocene Era. People smoked in buildings! People copied things on mimeograph machines and got high on the smell of the paper. Personal computers were the size and approximate shape of a clown car.

Jim liked to call me one of the Young Turks. I *knew* what Young Turk means, but I really didn't know what the etymology of the term was. As it turns out, the Young Turks were a group of young Turks a long time ago. Of course, they were *more* than that, or else it would be a stupid and meaningless term. At the beginning of the twentieth century, the Young Turks sought to rejuvenate the Turkish nation. The Young Turks are not young anymore and not even Turkish. They're dust.

Still, I wonder how this term, so localized and specific in meaning, traveled all the way to the twenty-first century, losing its context and most of its meaning along the way. I suppose such terms as "Young Turk" are plaques of a kind, commemorating something long forgotten. Not that anyone calls anyone else a Young Turk anymore. The last time I heard the phrase was probably the day Jim said it, referring to me.

I only remember one of my conversations with Jim. He criticized a minor point in a story of mine, the way a child narrator remembered the accent of an Appalachian man. I had written "kate." Jim said it would more accurately be represented as "cain't." Of course, he was right. I remember blowing him off, saying something like, "Thanks, Jim. I'll be sure to fix that." And I never did.

The next day, when I came to school, the office staff looked stricken. I asked the front office secretary what was wrong. "Did you hear?" she said almost in a whisper, "Jim BLANK had a heart attack and died last night."

"Jim BLANK?" I said. "Really? That's terrible," I said this because that's what we say when terrible things happen.

Everything happens for a reason. When one door closes, another one opens.

The English Department, wanting to commemorate Jim in some way, decided that the best way to honor Jim was to commission a plaque, complete with his photo, and install it in the corner of the hallway between the copying room and the front office where Jim hung out smoking every day. The plaque had Jim's picture on it in the manner of modern-day gravestones with photos of the Smiling Dead. Jim, smiling like he, too, was happy to be gone but not forgotten, was installed in that spot on the wall, and his plaque read JIM'S CORNER. Below, in smaller print were the words "Jim BLANK," and his dates, SOMETIME OR ANOTHER EARLIER IN THE CENTURY TO NOT QUITE THE TURN OF THE MILLENNIUM. I'd like to think there was some quote etched into the plaque, but I don't think there was. Something meaningful like:

What Goes Around Comes Around

Or:

Follow Your Bliss

Or:

"It's 'Cain't,' not 'Kate.'"

But nothing. Just plain and simple.

Jim's Corner.

Maybe the plaque didn't even list his dates. Not even a last name. Just his photo and the words "Jim's Corner" as though the corner would last generations and throngs would visit and know the feats of Jim, the corner on which he stood, and what he stood for, no explanation necessary.

Oddly, it worked for me. Every time I passed Jim's Corner, I thought of Jim, his smiling face, his words of wisdom, his brand of cigarette.

Years passed. Maybe six or seven and I left my job in Charlotte and found a new job on the West Coast. Just my luck. The year I left, the English Department moved to a new building. Our old offices, built in the German Pillbox Bunker Revival style of the late sixties and early seventies, no windows, and walls of cinderblock, were replaced with actual office spaces in which one might want to sit rather than flee to the hall by the copy machine and puff one's lungs out until one's heart gave way and one was rewarded with a plaque and a corner of eternity. The new office building looked nice, at least as nice was defined in the midnineties. A year or so later, I returned to Charlotte to give a reading in this new building. Afterward, I took a friend and former colleague aside. "You're going to think this is really strange," I said. "But I was wondering what happened to the plaque with Jim BLANK's name on it?"

My friend smiled sadly at me. "I knew you were going to ask about that. When we moved to the new building, we didn't take the plaque."

That made sense. You couldn't move Jim's Corner, of course. You couldn't put his likeness in a new building he didn't even live to see and designate some new virgin spot, untainted by cigarette smoke or copier fumes, as Jim's Corner. It wouldn't be right. But I at least hoped they'd left him where he hung, though I'm not sure why I felt so invested. I mean, I'd had about ten conversations with the guy before he died, all of them as forgettable as his last name. I'm sure it had something to do with my own fears. How soon would they forget me? How soon would memory swallow me so completely that not even a plaque with my name could raise a sad nod of remembrance?

"The space belongs to Criminal Justice now," my friend told me. "They took down the plaque."

"Do you know what they did with it?" I asked. "Did they at least send it to Jim's family?"

"I don't know," he said. "It's probably in a storeroom or else they simply threw it away."

I didn't want to hear that. Even though I hate plaques, I'm still fixated on the commemoration of people who are now mostly forgotten: family, friends, acquaintances, and strangers alike.

I used to look for the most obscure books by the most obscure authors and read them, and sometimes I'd make amazing discoveries. I thought I was keeping these people alive somehow in reading their words, the thoughts they had chosen to record as their own memorials.

One spring day, while still living in North Carolina, I came across a book sale given by the library. In the stacks of books offered for sale, I found a remarkable collection of poetry from the 1960s. Chapbooks by Kenneth Rexroth and Gary Snyder. Issues of obscure literary magazines from England and America. On the inside flap of each cover was the name Amon Liner. I wondered who this Amon Liner was, and so I asked a colleague who'd taught at the university since the late '60s.

He flipped through one of the books I bought and expressed surprise that the books had been offered for sale. Amon Liner, he explained, had been a promising poet in Charlotte who had died young of a terminal disease. His mother had donated Amon's papers and book collection in good faith to the university library, expecting the books to be preserved, but now they were selling his books for a dollar a dozen. What could I do but return to the sale and buy the rest of Amon Liner's forlorn collection? Of course, buying Amon's books did nothing—it didn't bring him back, it didn't make him live. But still, I saw it as some form of expiation, though even now I'm not sure what I sought expiation for. I still haven't read any of Amon's books. In the four moves since I bought them, I think I left some of them behind, resold some, donated others. The only reason I still remember Amon's name is because it's so unusual, and every time I see his handwriting in one of his dwindling books, I try to imagine the hand that signed it, the body, the face, the personality, the poems attached to that hand, but now none of it remains, of course, except that name, hidden in a book, returned to a corner of my bookshelf: *Amon's Corner*. Is it his secret plaque? And where will mine be located, if at all?

A plaque located between the moving sidewalk and the train inside the C Concourse at the Cincinnati Airport reads:

> *In memory of Robert Allen whose twelve years of dedicated service were instrumental in the construction of this facility. 1935–1993.*

A Smiling Dead photo etched into the plaque shows a guy in his midfifties with a bad toupee. He's dressed for some special occasion (maybe a high school reunion? a daughter's marriage?), in a tux with a carnation in the lapel.

He is in the perfect location to be completely ignored as people rush by on the way to their flights:

"Attention. You are approaching the end of the moving sidewalk. Watch your step as you leave the moving sidewalk."

Who did the people who put up this plaque think they were fooling? Did they actually believe people would stop, risk missing their flights, and meditate with gratitude on Robert Allen's twelve years of service? Well, at least I did, though only out of morbid curiosity and because I had some time to kill. Still, I wonder why plaques are so often located in spots where people rush by, in spots not exactly conducive to meditation or else squirreled away in forgotten nooks?

A historical marker I used to pass every day in Charlotte on my way to the university sat on a small median in the middle of a busy highway. In order to reach it, one had to park one's car on the shoulder and dash across several lanes of traffic to reach what some group, some Daughters of the This or That thought so damned important it was worth risking one's own life to read. I suppose the highway has simply grown up around the plaque by now, as though History shat where it thought it wouldn't be observed and out came a historical marker.

Jim . . . Jim . . . what was his last name? No matter how hard I try, I can't remember, though it's somewhere there, always just out of reach.

Some years ago, while waiting for the elevator in College Hall, an early nineteenth-century building on the campus of Vermont College of Fine Arts, I noticed a plaque recording the academic excellence of the campus dorms from the years 1964 to 1970. In 1964, the students of Bishop Hall won the Scholastic Achievement Award. Three out of the four years from 1966 through 1969, the residents of Glover captured this glorious honor, until it was wrested away by the residents of Harris Hall, the last students ever to hold this prize. From this point on, there's plenty of room, but no winners, simply small gold blanks waiting forever to have names etched upon them. Vermont College began in the 1830s as a theological seminary, and one can see the reason for hanging photos of the seminary music society, literary society, and baseball teams from the 1800s—they invite contemplation. As one gazes into the confident faces of these Young Turks, one has at least an intimation of their lives.

Susan Sontag writes, "As photographs give people an imaginary posses-sion of a past that is unreal, they also help people to take possession of space in which they are insecure." But plaques do no such thing. In me, they do the opposite, creating insecurity in a space in which I previously felt secure. They memorialize a person or a place often without context and in a way that attempts a sense of permanence (and rarely succeeds). Photos don't give such false reassurance. They speak of loss even as they give us a sense of continuity with the past.

Recently, Vermont College partnered with Colorado College in Boulder and moved away from Montpelier. Certainly, no one will give a thought to the many plaques for achievements past for a college that no longer exists, and why should they? A new coat of paint will take care of any shadows of the plaques that once graced those halls.

Hedges. That was his last name. Jim Hedges. This, for a moment, is his new corner.

Over time, a plaque simply becomes something one never notices. A plaque is the location of our own anxiety about death and erasure. Its very existence is its own negation. Your eyes run over it. Why should you care? You're about to step on the moving sidewalk.

In the Theater of Half-Truths

> It is this kind of question that Photography raises for me: questions which
> derive from a "stupid" or simple metaphysics (it is the answers which are
> complicated): probably the true metaphysics.
> —Roland Barthes, *Camera Lucida*

One reason photographs speak to me is because of their very muteness.
I, who cannot keep quiet, feel compelled to listen to them. I can't resist
interpreting photographs because of their lack of resistance to interpretation, from the most documentary photo to the most stylized. Photographs cannot defend themselves, and even the image that seems to tell
the starkest tale—say, a photograph of the liberation of Auschwitz—can
be denied, reinterpreted, reinvented. Only those who were at Auschwitz
or their liberators can speak for the photo, can say that this really happened and was not staged for the camera or otherwise manipulated by
the photographer. Once all the eyewitnesses have died (and, of course,
eyewitness accounts are often less definitive than photographs) then we
only have our own moral certitude to fall back on, at least if we're relying
only on the photograph for documentary evidence, and not other types
of records. Photographs are witnesses, but not foolproof ones. Battlefield
photographs have in some cases been staged for almost as long as photography has existed. Civil War photographer Matthew Brady often arrived
at battlefields long after the battle had taken place and at least in several
instances posed his assistants as corpses. The aim wasn't to fool the public

so much as to inform the public, to give his viewers a whiff of battle. Is there anything wrong with this?

All peopled photographs are theater, even those that are candid. Portraits, snapshots, documentary photos, stylized or self-conscious artistic photos, certainly authors' photos—all theater of a kind, some more theatrical than others. But by their very nature, their muteness, their stopping of time, they constitute an ambiguous kind of drama. John Berger, writing of the "language of appearances," claims that images tend to "cohere." So when I see a photo of a baby at its mother's breast, my memories and expectations combine to create an idea of this baby, both at once particular and generalized. This is in part why the photo of a complete stranger can move me. Through memory and expectation, I supply a kind of mini narrative.

I'd call it theatrical rather than story-like or even cinematic because of the static quality of the photo and the set of the theater stage, but for other reasons as well. The fourth wall in theater is the audience. The fourth wall in the photograph is the viewer, who in turn becomes an actor in the drama.

Actors attempt to understand their role by investigating the motivations of their character. In a person-centered photograph, the viewer is as much concerned with text and subtext as an actor is. What does the photo say through its appearances, and what does it *really* say? The viewer, in this case, steps into the photo and becomes the actor for a moment in the mini drama, based on memory and expectation. We can and do sympathize with people who have been injured, massacred, displaced, as depicted in photos, but as Susan Sontag points out, this sympathy often takes the place of action, a moral passivity that allows us just as easily to move on to the next photo in the series, muttering, "How horrible," and leaving it at that. And the dramas enacted by even the most horrific photographs are contained within the walls of the photo, often leaving out details that might complicate the actor's role.

Step into Eddie Adams's famous photo of the South Vietnamese general executing a suspected member of the communist guerrillas, the Vietcong, on the streets of Saigon. You might think you know the role well—there's a villain and there's a victim. But Adams felt conflicted about this photograph and wound up feeling more sympathy for the executioner than the victim. Of photographs in general he writes: "Still photographs are the most powerful weapon in the world. People believe them, but photographs do lie, even without manipulation. They are only half-truths." This famous photo leaves out the circumstances of the street execution. In the photo, General Nguyen Ngoc Loan is caught in the moment of shooting a Vietcong prisoner, Nguyen Van Lem. Loan, the chief of the National Police of South Vietnam, was reacting in a moment of rage to the murder of Colonel Nguyễn Tuân, along with the colonel's wife, six of their children, and the colonel's eighty-year-old mother. A murder allegedly carried out by several Vietcong, Lem among them. A seventh child was wounded but survived by lying quietly beside his mother as she bled to death. Later, this child, wounded three times in the attack that killed his family, was adopted in the U.S. and became the highest ranking Vietnamese American in the military, a Rear Admiral. What enraged Loan and made him raise his gun to Lem's temple was not the massacre in itself, but the fact that Lem was not wearing a uniform. To Loan, Lem's act was cowardly because as a guerrilla, not dressed in a military uniform, he could simply blend in with other civilians after committing his act.

Some claim that the execution was a photo op, that it was staged. Regardless, the photo became a stage like all such photos, the viewer walking onto that stage and assuming the role they think is self-evident. Like all dramas, the photo of the street execution takes place at the crossroads of experience, expectation, and imagination. The experience upon which the drama is based has long since disappeared and what is left is an interpretation, a revival of the original.

One of the chief delights of photographs is their confounding natures, the fact that we often want them to open up a keyhole to history, to authenticity, when they only open up a keyhole to ourselves.

Photographs are inexorably linked to our desire for authenticity. Take for example the crowds at the Louvre hovering around the Mona Lisa, snapping photos above their heads, hardly aiming, as though the Mona Lisa were a starlet and they were paparazzi who might turn their fuzzy snapshots into millions of dollars. The lure of authenticity seems as irresistible as the gravitational pull of a dead star. Don DeLillo captured this type of moment marvelously in *White Noise* when his protagonist visits the "most

Fig. 2. People clamor to take a photo of the Mona Lisa in the Louvre. Paul Swinney / Alamy Stock Photo.

photographed barn in America," the quintessential American barn, so photographed that no one sees the actual barn anymore, but simply its representation. Of course, such encounters are about symbolic possession, but they're also about drama. The quadrillionth photographer of the Mona Lisa seeks to be part of the drama of the Mona Lisa. Such photos hold no allure for anyone besides the person who took them and perhaps their immediate family. In the language of appearances, the idea of the Mona Lisa is so general that it can no longer be particularized except by the person who took the quadrillionth photo of it. But the photographer is happy. They look at their photo and enter for a moment into the photograph of the painting. They step from the chorus to leading actor for a moment. Their role has been elevated above the rest of the visitors thronging the famous painting. The camera here becomes a tool of anxiety about the photographer's place in the world.

Camera Lucida was Roland Barthes's last book, written not long after his mother died. The book is an elegy for his mother camouflaged as a book on theory. He describes searching for a photo of his mother shortly after she died, one that would capture her essence. For the most part, the search was fruitless until he came upon a photo of her and her brother as young children standing on a bridge in a glass conservatory. He calls it the Winter Garden photo. When the photo was taken, his mother's parents were going through a divorce. He describes the photo but refuses to reproduce it in his book. He writes: "I cannot reproduce the Winter Garden Photograph. It exists only for me. For you, it would be nothing but an indifferent picture, one of the thousand manifestations of the 'ordinary' . . ."

He couldn't be more wrong. In fact, his description is so poignant that of all the photos in *Camera Lucida*, it's the one I best remember.

It *is* true literally that a photograph shows a person as the self they never see. As we know, but don't necessarily process when we look in the mirror, the reflection we see is a reversed image. A photographer told me that when he was first starting out, he sometimes took portraits of people who hated the way they looked in photos. As a solution, he started flipping the negatives, and invariably the problem was solved, and the client felt comfortable again with the self they saw.

In a studio shot, the customer has the right to accept or reject, to pose as they want. The same holds true for nearly every smiling tourist photo ever taken. Here, the subject symbolically possesses the camera if not the photographer. Far from predatory, the camera becomes a tool of the actor's trade.

The biggest act is the formal portrait. I love to study them, from the stacks of anonymous nineteenth-century portraits you can find in antique stores to my own family's portraits through the years to my own author's portraits on the books I've written. My mother had an author friend in New York, Ursule Molinaro, who refused to allow photos of herself on her book jackets. My mother thought Ursule didn't want her soul snatched away, but I think she was simply being smart. My own jacket photos cause me nothing but shame now, so clearly do I see the Idea of Author I was trying to portray, and badly, with each successive book. As time passes, the subject of a portrait will invariably come to regard it as the expression of a failed role.

"I was so young then!"

"I can't believe I wore my hair like that!"

"Who did I think I was fooling?"

In *Remote: Reflections on Life in the Shadow of Celebrity*, David Shields slyly illustrates the act of the formal portrait in a section titled "About the Author," in which he places his book jacket photos side by side, instantly parodying himself while simultaneously redeeming himself by the very self-awareness this juxtaposing of selves implies.

When I was writing my memoir about my older sister Nola, who died at the age of twenty-five, I consciously inserted photographs into the text as I was writing the book and formed the words around photos. This was 1997—the ability to do this on one's computer and not immediately run out of memory (no pun intended) was a relatively recent innovation. For me, the photograph was as much talisman as evidence. The photos I used were as much magical evocations as illustrations or authentications. I wanted some essence of the people I had loved to infuse me and the words I wrote about them. I wanted to reach back into the past and snatch them, carrying them into the temporary haven of the present. I wanted to comfort and be comforted, trouble and be troubled, and in large part it worked. Berger calls the language of appearances "oracular." And it was true for me that these photographs spoke in an oracular manner, sometimes faintly, sometimes in ways that needed interpretation.

Time elevates memory in the same way that time elevates photographs. A fixed memory from childhood fascinates us the older we get. Sometimes we have no idea why the memory survives—not necessarily an important moment from childhood, maybe as simple a memory as stepping off a bus at the age of five and looking up into the sunlit branches of a tree. What is remarkable about that moment? Perhaps nothing except that it has survived. Perhaps more, but it's there that we need to investigate, contemplate, burrow. We need to learn how to speak for the fixed images of memory.

As Akiko Busch points out in *The Uncommon Life of Common Objects*, digital photography works as memory does because it edits and erases in the same manner as memory. The memoir and the digital photograph share a great deal in common—the digital photograph employs a kind of willful selectivity and invention that mirrors in many ways the memoirist's process. A child in a wading pool in the background gets erased because she doesn't fit the program of the photographer or the program of the memoirist, either for aesthetic reasons, reasons of privacy, or reasons of psychological sensitivity.

One image that leaps to mind from my memoir and from memory is a studio portrait of my mother in the late 1940s, taken by the famous New York photographer Aaron Siskind. Few photographs could seem more stylized than this. My mother, in her early thirties, looks every bit the glamorous

·   JUN   ·   69

Fig. 3. The Kortlanders, 1969. Credit: Photo taken by William Kortlander, used by permission of John Kortlander.

author as she wanted to be. The photo Siskind took of my mother was an advertisement of her, a refinement of how she wanted to be seen, making her not only an object but a product.

Not long ago, I was chatting with some acquaintances when one of them asked simply what a face is. The question took us by surprise—it seemed an odd, obvious question and at the same time the type of thing too easily taken for granted. Well, it's the place we like to keep our noses, mouths, and eyes, of course. Everyone present took the bait, and stammered, trying to describe what a face is rather than simply what it does. I don't remember what most of the answers were, but I remember someone saying that a face is a mask. I knew *that* wasn't the right answer. At best, the face is a lot of masks, not simply one. A mask is a representation of a face and so when someone calls a face a mask, they're saying in effect that a face is a representation of a face that is a representation of a face, ad infinitum.

For me, a face is a stage on which emotion plays. The camera produces a number of dramas upon this stage, each a separate performance.

In trying to understand why some images fascinate and others don't,

Roland Barthes devises in *Camera Lucida* an eccentric yet appealing method for explaining his interest or lack of interest in a particular photograph. It's what he terms the *"punctum"* and the *"studium."* The studium, as Barthes explains it, is a photo or a part of a photo that holds a kind of dispassionate or historical interest for the reader. The punctum, by contrast, is what fascinates us, though "fascinate" is too mild a term. What wounds us, the wound of the photo, is the way Barthes phrases it. A photo of three soldiers patrolling in Nicaragua is all studium to Barthes because, in the background of this photo, we see two nuns crossing the street. The elements of the photo are easily grasped, too easily, and so it holds no interest for Barthes. Another photo shows a gathering of smiling kids in Little Italy in 1954. A toy gun is pressed by someone taller and older to the temple of one smiling boy's head. Here, the punctum, the wound of the photo, for Barthes is not the gun but the boy's bad teeth. It's a detail, a tiny shock. In another photo of Queen Victoria on horseback, she's all studium to Barthes while the kilted groom holding the bridle is punctum. Don't try to understand this concept rationally, because it's not meant to be rational but a reaction, a private reaction.

He writes of one photo:

> Here is Queen Victoria photographed in 1863 by George W. Wilson; she is on horseback, her skirt suitably draping the entire animal (this is the historical interest, the *studium*); but beside her, attracting my eyes, a kilted groom holds the horse's bridle; this is the *punctum*; for even I do not know just what the social status of this Scotsman may be (servant? Equerry?) I can see his function clearly: to supervise the horse's behavior.

It's easy to explain in different terms why Barthes was so fascinated with this photo, leaving aside the punctum and studium. Barthes neglects to describe the expressions on the faces of Victoria and her kilted "groomsman." Hers is bland and blank. His is intense, intent, guarded, guarding. He looks as though he will reach through the mists of time and throttle you if you dare approach the Queen. And, indeed, he *would* do so if he could. While Barthes does not know the identity of this man, I do. His name was John Brown and he was the subject of the 1997 film *Mrs. Brown*, starring Judi Dench and Billy Connolly, about the devotion and dependence Victoria and Brown had for one another. One look at Brown in this photo and you're mesmerized. All

Fig. 4. Queen Victoria with John Brown. GL Archive / Alamy Stock Photo.

punctum. But a plainer, less fanciful way to view our interest in the photo is in its elaborate staging and the inherent drama that it suggests to the viewer, whether or not the viewer knows anything at all about John Brown, or even Queen Victoria. Billy Connolly must have studied this photo for the role—in the film he was able to perfectly capture Brown's expressive intensity.

In John Berger and Jean Mohr's book *Another Way of Telling*, Swiss photographer Jean Mohr makes this point that we want photos to tell us what they're about, but they can't, so we speak for them. Mohr takes five photographs from his archives and shows them to a disparate group of people, asking them to essentially caption the photographs, to speak for them.

Some of the photos are more easily deciphered than others. A girl seemingly biting her doll is indeed biting her doll. But a young man floating among tree branches is only a photographer trying to get a better view of an anti-war demonstration in Washington, DC, in the early 1970s. A man with his arms spread wide is a Turkish worker in a German factory trying to get the photographer's attention. The supplied explanations dismiss our interest in the photos' narratives. If we remain enamored of them, it's most likely because of their formal composition, the visual coherence of the photos. But the photos that are most haunting narratively are the two outside my normal ken at least, one of a figure asleep on a giant pipeline and a group of twenty-five or thirty men from South Asia, dressed in T-shirts for the most part, staring solemnly at the viewer. In these two cases, the explanations provided by the photographer are just as intriguing, if not more, than those I might supply with my imagination. One photo shows a group of Sri Lankan men who are listening to a presentation about the benefits of vasectomies. The other photo is of a boy outside of Mumbai lying on a pipe bringing water to the city—the pipes are cool and he's done it to escape the heat. To someone in Mumbai or Sri Lanka, these photos might seem utterly pedestrian and the photo of the young man in the flowering tree truly exotic. We can't control what appeals to us in a photograph—though a photo often makes public a private moment, it still remains a kind of private visual correspondence between the photo and the viewer. What the viewer brings to the viewing—imagination and their private associations and memory—can't necessarily be rationally explained.

One of the many reasons W. G. Sebald's novels are so fascinating is the way he blurs the boundaries between the aims of authentication, illustration, and evocation in the photos with which he peppers his narratives. The black-and-white photos of the eastern shore of England in *The Rings of Saturn* seem like illustrations at first, but illustrations to what effect? The photos for the most part depict the most ordinary scenes, largely unpeopled.

The photographs in his work confound our expectations of what a photo should do (I wonder if Barthes would see only studium in Sebald's photos) *and* what a novel should do. Photographs illustrating a novel? Doesn't that make it nonfiction? Despite or because of their ambiguous natures, Sebald's photos have on the reader the same *talismanic* effect that the photos in my memoir had for me. They are meant not to evoke an exterior landscape but an interior one.

I don't mean to compete with Barthes, but as long as we're assigning Latin words to photos, allow me to offer something in between, or complementary at least, to punctum and studium. I am interested in what I might refer to as the *telesma* of the photograph. A photo can be all studium as in Sebald's washed-out landscapes and still possess telesma. These photos seem magical in their ability to transcend time or in their complex, sometimes contradictory evocations of the human drama. The telesma is that talismanic aspect of the image that draws us into it. The photo that possesses telesma doesn't ward off evil spirits per se, but time and mortality. It invites us, even traps us, in some place between ambiguity and awe. It is that which astonishes us. "In themselves appearances are ambiguous, with multiple meanings" writes Berger. "This is why the visual is astonishing and why memory based on the visual, is freer than reason." Some photos possess telesma close to the surface, almost bubbling out of them. Some require a little investigation before you discover the telesma. The first photograph ever taken, between 1826 and 1827, depicts rooftops taken from a second-story window. A similar photo taken today would likely be cast off as a mistake by a photographer, but this photo possesses telesma—there is something undeniably magical in it being the first.

If you disbelieve that something is magical, it loses its power. It ceases to astonish. If you believe a photo of Matthew Brady's Civil War dead was staged, your skepticism will likely, though not necessarily, diminish the photo's telesma. A new window of telesma might open up for you as you imagine the scene of the assistants posing as dead on that long ago afternoon, and all of them long since turned to dust. Similarly, in a portrait, its very staginess creates its own telesma, especially as time passes and the role the actor played in the portrait seems ever more pathetic and vulnerable. And what of purposefully staged artistic photos, such as Cindy Sherman's and other

Fig. 5. The world's first photographic image: Joseph Nicéphore Niépce (French, 1765–1833), *Untitled 'point de vue,'* 1827. Heliograph on pewter, 16.7 x 20.3 x .15 cm. Gernsheim Collection, purchase, 964:0000:000, Harry Ransom Center, The University of Texas at Austin.

artists whose work plays with melodrama and movie moments? These photos are cultural talismans of a kind—for me, they are curious, even remarkable in their effects of simulation and satire, but I can't discern the telesma in them. Their very pointedness, the fact that they speak so unambiguously in the language of appearances, robs them of telesma for me. Another way of putting it: the drama of such photos seems exhausted.

Other photographs may be granted telesma by the viewer, may be salvaged from becoming "an indifferent picture, one of the thousand manifestations of the 'ordinary.'" While photo captions often try to fix meaning in a photo in a way that is ultimately futile and unsatisfying, writers of imagination do the opposite. They create a mix of image and language that can take the blandest photograph and turn it into a talisman against the very forces of banality and mortality with which photographer and subject and viewer all struggle.

One does not even need the photograph itself to grant it telesma, but simply the memory of the photograph. Take, for example, Barthes's own description of the unrevealed Winter Garden photo:

Alone in the apartment where his mother had died, Barthes one day sorted through photographs of her one by one under the light of a lamp, scouring each picture for a glimpse of the person he had loved, gradually traveling back in time with her. And then he discovered a photograph unlike all the others. The faded sepia print showed his mother when she was only five years old standing with her seven-year-old brother on a wooden bridge in a glassed-in conservatory:

> He was leaning against the bridge railing, along which he had extended one arm; she, shorter than he, was standing a little back, facing the camera; you could tell that the photographer had said, "Step forward a little so we can see you"; she was holding one finger in the other hand, as children often do, in an awkward gesture. The brother and sister, united, as I knew, by the discord of their parents, who were soon to divorce, had posed side by side, alone, under the palms of the Winter Garden . . .

In this photograph, Barthes at last discovers his mother, in the distinctness of her face, the docile place she has assumed beside her brother, the innocence of her face and gestures, what he refers to as a "sovereign innocence."

Here, Barthes's language becomes a reliquary for the image. Barthes has granted the photograph telesma in his lovely evocation of it and need not reproduce it for us because he has fixed it in our minds the way he wants us to see it, with the same reverence and magic it contains for him. It's no coincidence that commentators on photography continually speak of magic when trying to understand the photograph: "the oracular nature of appearance," as Berger says; "a magic, not an art" . . . "prophecy in reverse," says Barthes; "the magic of the real," Sontag calls it.

In Lawrence Sutin's book *A Postcard Memoir*, Sutin illustrates this idea of telesma in a fashion completely differently than Barthes's search for his mother. In this book, Sutin uses images from his vast collection of nineteenth- and early twentieth-century postcards and employs them in ways they were certainly never meant, as touchstones for meditations on his own life. The reproduced postcards and meditations, side by side on the page, are not explanations. Through his words, Sutin sees the subjects of the photos in ways they never could, and more importantly, sees himself through the photographs in a way he perhaps never could without them.

Once a photograph has been taken, it's not inviolable. It's not the end of the story. The photo from another era seems to carry a drama within it, but the exact nature of that drama often remains opaque.

The word "reliquary" strikes me as just right in trying to understand this. The bone of a saint, by its very nature, possesses telesma, but without the reliquary to contain it, what's to distinguish it from any other ordinary bone? Sometimes, a photograph alone serves as a reliquary for human experience. Sometimes, language alone serves as a reliquary. And sometimes, employing both language and the image, another form of reliquary is created. Transcendent magic and mortal drama. These are the cornerstones of human existence, and it is at the confounding intersections of the two where the photograph haunts me.

In the Storeroom of Figments

A walking stick made from a bull's penis. A cup cooler made from its testicles. The Omni Talking Robot. A recumbent bicycle to lie on and pedal three lazy revolutions down the hall and back. One of the first CD players ever made, straight from SONY Japan, not to be taken home, not to be lost, not to be stolen or borrowed—not even by any of the three bosses, Jim, Ed, or David, the Uber boss. Polo cologne, Armani. Burberry. These can be borrowed, stolen, taken home, even by the lowest of the low in the Modern Living Department, the Control Clerk. What does that title mean? Control Clerk. He tells friends that he controls all the clerks if they get into the building. It's a stupid joke, but it made someone laugh once, and so he says it over and over. His office, in the *Playboy* building in Chicago, is the repository for everything hip and odd. The epicenter of cultural instability, the place where sexual desire married the urge to be hip, not odd. But the big joke is this: Mr. Hip always becomes odd over time. Mr. Hip sprouts hairs on his back, from his ears. Mr. Hip dyes his hair, develops an allergy to deodorant, gets that old man smell, still thinks "Soap on a Rope" is cool. Over time, he can't control the clerks any longer. He looks in the mirror. The clerks have taken over his world. They rock his world. They lick his ears with their sandpaper tongues. He listens to Michael Jackson's "Thriller" at night, his little alarm clock. *Wake up*, Michael says, sprawled in white and Jerri-curls across the album cover. *You're not hip. You're odd, like me.*

On the L to his job during morning rush hour, the Control Clerk sees a man wearing a single glove like Michael wears. The man looks poor, in his early thirties. The one-gloved hand holds the pole to steady him as he looks solemnly ahead, lost in some dream of himself as not himself. Years later, the Control Clerk will purchase a Hamsa, the Hand of God, and wear it around his neck. He will not remember the man on the L when he makes the purchase, but he remembers the man now. He remembers the man because he thought the man was the sorriest human he'd ever seen, pretending to be Michael Jackson when he clearly was not, when Michael Jackson did not concern himself with the desires or fate of the man on the L, except perhaps in the most abstract sense.

The Control Clerk thinks a lot of things are funny about his job. He thinks it's funny that on St. Patrick's Day and Valentine's Day, thirteen or so drunks invariably try to sneak into the *Playboy* building in search of Miss March, as though she lives here at 919 North Michigan Ave. But she doesn't. She lives nowhere near here. She is as much a figment in the *Playboy* building as she is in the muzzled minds of the drunks who get caught in the stairwells. A stack of her resides in the storeroom up on the tenth floor, editorial. The Control Clerk goes there often in search of back issues because his bosses sometimes need them for reference or to send to a client. Go ahead and steal these. It's fine. The corporate culture of *Playboy* encourages thievery because what honor can there be in working for *Playboy*, really? Even in 1983, maybe especially then, everyone is looking for something to steal, to borrow, to abscond with. No one really takes the job seriously except for a few Mr. Hips in Editorial who really seem to believe there's such a thing as a *Playboy* Male. Even at the age of twenty-three, the Control Clerk knows there's no such thing as the *Playboy* Male, and that's what makes him secretly hipper than all those editors at *Playboy* who believe they're so cool. He wears his hipness like a rhinestone-studded glove, turned inside out. No, there's no such thing as the *Playboy* Male, though plenty of pretenders: Asa and Kurt and Bill, the guy who talks about his motocross trips across Mongolia as though he needs to impress a twenty-three-year-old Control Clerk. The funny thing is this: he *does* need to impress a twenty-three-year-old Control Clerk. Forty-year-old *Playboy* Males live to impress twenty-three-year-old nothing males who hold the key to the storeroom where the figments are stored.

■

A variation on the story of the tiger and the maiden. Behind one door lies a voluptuous maiden. Behind another, thirteen drunks in the stairwell who don't know the code to reenter the building. The drunks are banging on the door, toppling down the stairs and shaking with delirium tremens. They long to get behind the door with the maiden. But if they succeed in opening the stairwell (it's only a three-number code, how hard can it be?), they find another door, and they join thirteen more drunks instead of one lovely maiden; now there are twenty-six of them crowded into another stairwell of the *Playboy* building. And they do this again and again until their numbers become crushing, the air fetid, and someone pities them and lets them out of the stairwell, finally, and onto the street, and they make the long sour-smelling journey home on the L, past the man with his one glove who thinks he's better than they are, more connected to his fantasies, or they remain in the stairwell forever, which is almost always the case, and which is known henceforward as "The Storeroom of *Playboy* Males."

We do not go there often. But we are here now.

■

The *Playboy* building?
   That's right.
   What do you do at *Playboy*?
   I'm a . . . an editorial assistant.
   Yeah? That so? You give the bunnies massages and stuff?
   Ha ha. Yes, I give bunnies massages.
   Seriously. You ever meet a bunny?
   Well no, not really. I'm in the Modern Living Department. We handle everything that isn't flesh.
   You mean, like the electronics and shit?

Yeah, that's right. Record players. Really advanced record players. Stuff you've never seen before. CD players—

So you never see the bunnies?

Yeah, I see them all the time. Same as you. You can keep the change.

⁘

The *Playboy* Male, circa 1983:

He is serving a life sentence in Joliette for aggravated murder during a convenience store hold-up gone terribly wrong.

He is the fifty-three-year-old guy out in Glen Ellyn who bought the first issue of *Playboy* thirty years ago and matches the satin gloss of the centerfold with the shininess of his bald spot. Around this time, it is decreed that age is a state of mind, you're only as old as you feel, and that old ladies will wear purple. *Wear all the purple you want*, he thinks. *It changes nothing.*

He is the guy from Puerto Rico who has sent a letter to the guy who rides motorcycles across Mongolia. The guy who rides motorcycles across Mongolia thinks it's hilarious, so he copies the letter and lets everyone in the *Playboy* building, from the mailroom to the Control Clerk, read it so that they can all share a laugh at such a loser. The letter even makes its way to the fifth floor of the *Playboy* building where the Denizens of Modern Living lurk.

> Dear *Playboy*,
>
> I apply to be a male model for you and I think you want me. I smoke the cigarettes and drink what you sell in the pages of *Playboy Magazine* and I think I am the idea of what you guys want to show the world. Am average height and build and weight and good looking. Please let me know to start.

There's talk of sending the letter to Hef out in California at the Mansion, but it's only talk. "God, it would break his heart," David, the head of Modern Living says, snickering sadly. There is such a thing as a sad snicker. David specializes in them. "Are you kidding?" The guy who rides Mongolia shouts. "Hef would shit a brick laughing." This is how honest-to-God *Playboy* Males talk to one another. Shit a brick. A euphemism best left back in 1983.

Perhaps David, the Uber boss, is the avatar of the *Playboy* Male. He seems to love the place. *He* could have written that letter himself thirty years ago. He's in his late forties or early fifties and sports (that's the right word, "sports!") a silver beard, neatly trimmed. His voice is pitched somewhere between Larry and Curly of the Three Stooges, high but not *that* high. Not underwear-too-tight-sperm-count-low high.

Hef famously pads around at all hours of the day and night in his famous bathrobe. He has never set foot in the Modern Living corridor on the fifth floor, never seen the bull's penis walking stick, or the Omni Talking Robot, most likely never tasted a beer cooled in the scrotum of a bull. The only aspect of the magazine that interests him anymore is the comics section. David reports he's addicted to "Little Orphan Fanny." This is why morale is so low at *Playboy*—he's sent in a girl (!), his daughter, Christie, to be the leader while he skips around in his pee-stained PJs at *Playboy* Mansion West. But everyone here respects Christie, who wears business suits and looks freshly MBA-scrubbed. The Control Clerk thinks about her constantly. She has blond, permed hair, a small nose. She wears an A-cup and her turn-ons are:

Aussie accents

Mad Max movies

Pac-Man

A guy who can whisper kinky things in Eastern bloc languages, particularly Russian and Polish.

Favorite Movie: *Zhivago*, of course! You silly Control Clerk!

Favorite Book, *The Art of War* by Sun Tzu.

This profile is distributed by the Control Clerk to all visitors upon entrance to the *Playboy* building. Memorized by all employees. Recited by children throughout greater Chicagoland instead of the Pledge of Allegiance.

The Control Clerk has had exactly two dealings with Christie Hefner. He wrote her a memo asking *Playboy* to send NPR some money as part of *Playboy*'s commitment to free speech. She wrote back a polite note saying it was a good suggestion and thanks, but NPR didn't quite fit the profile of *Playboy*'s donations. He also saw her at the company Halloween party. She was dressed as a geisha.

■

Morale is kind of low at *Playboy*. Maybe because of Hef deserting the Hef-house. He left the *Playboy* Mansion a few years back after one of his aides killed herself. Don't think she was his lover, though she might have had a crush on him. She wasn't beautiful, wasn't up to snuff, so maybe that's why she snuffed herself. Snuff films. Another 1983 commodity—films that combine sex and death, as if they don't all. Some are real, most not.

He doesn't want to return to Chicago. Too many bad memories, and life is too short, eh? To walk around in your bathrobe all day in a cold gray city that allows such unhappiness? And his first wife is there too. She's a receptionist. She's been a receptionist at *Playboy* since almost the beginning. When she was young and beautiful, Hef loved her enough to marry her and give her a daughter named Christie. Her name is Carol and she works for her daughter now. She works for her ex-husband. She works for *Playboy* Males the world over. She answers the phone, "*Playboy*. How may I direct your call?" And then she puts them on hold and they listen to "Only the Lonely" until they give up like the drunks in the stairwell. Her hair is gray and she always has a smile on her face. She is the subject of water-cooler conversation. Not because of anything she did, but because of what she failed to do.

No, Mr. Hef, we don't blame you, we love you, but you have left us behind in this windy heartless place where it's dark by late afternoon and the wind really does blow. Sometimes it howls and the Control Clerk once had to rescue an elderly woman from a pole she was clinging to desperately on North Michigan Avenue. She was old with purple veins, or so he imagines, but he rescued her anyway because that's what you would have done too, Mr. Hef.

The company is going down the boob tube. Everyone knows this. Everyone thinks Hef is off his rocker. He's only interested in comics, not even the famous *Playboy* interviews or the fiction, his last tenuous hold on respectability. Hef is wasting all his time and money on something called *The Playboy Channel* and *Playboy* videos. Everyone knows there's no future in that. *Playboy* never made a snuff film. Of course not. What people don't understand is that *Playboy* is the Disney of porn—they have more than bunnies in common. They even have theme parks in common, and within miles of one another in California.

■

People picket once or twice a week in front of the *Playboy* building and the Control Clerk has walked through the lines many times to enter the building. Feminists, the Religious Right too. The Control Clerk has never had a problem breaking the picket line. The picketers chant and never make eye contact with him.

We are not your playthings, Mr. Hefner, they shout.

O Sodomites, they yell, give yourself to God.

The picketers, on the left *and* the right, don't seem to realize one simple fact: *Playboy* in 1983 is to moral turpitude what Grenada is to the balance of world power.

■

Morale is high in the United States. We have just invaded the tiny island nation of Grenada and saved a bunch of American med students from partying too hard with communists. "All Night Long" is the song most often heard in the mailroom of the *Playboy* building, on the lowest floor, where all the workers are Black and unutterably happy. One day, the Control Clerk sees a twenty-dollar bill lying on the floor of the mailroom. He bends to pick it up and it jumps from his hand. He bends again and it jumps. One of the mail clerks emerges from behind the Coke machine, laughing uproariously. They high-five each other in the way that males do the world over to acknowledge and subvert humiliation at once, to express and divert domination. At Halloween, this same mail clerk dresses in the best costume by far, a many-segmented dragon that everyone is in awe of. Christie Hefner, as a geisha, allows no emotion to cross her face. She floats by after a few minutes. Back to work. Halloween is dead! Long live Halloween!

■

The Control Clerk worries that he is not happy. One day, as he's leaving the L on Chicago and State, emerging into the winter sunshine of Chicago, a hand with an iron grasp clamps his shoulder and he turns to see who it is, who has nearly brought him to his knees. But no one is there. He staggers to work and David tells him to go to the doctor, who tells him he's suffered an anxiety attack. "Anxiety can be physical like that?" he asks, naïve Control Clerk that he is. The doctor just smiles. Every physical object in the world is anxiety's shit, from rabbit-pellet-sized fortunes in fortune cookies, to the tallest building in the world, which in 1983 is the Sears Tower, dark monument to the world's anxiety over our inability to touch God. Of *course*, he suffered an anxiety attack. He works at Anxiety Central, trying to keep those clerks controlled, the drunks at bay, products from being stolen, borrowed, absconded with.

After putting in a year at *Playboy*, he earns a certificate of congratulations signed by Hef himself.

If not for the pictures on the wall, he tells others, you'd think you were working for the Kreamo Bread Company. Even some of the pictures are deceptive. There's a smiling, giggling baby. If you look closely, you can see it's jacking off under its diaper. And there are plenty of *Playboy*'s trademark long-legged Vargas girls on the walls. But nothing too graphic. *Playboy* has never really been about cocks and cunts. It's the caricature, the cartoon girl, the baby with its hand down its diaper. That baby, though unacknowledged, is the quintessential *Playboy* Male. He can't read the interviews. He just looks at the pictures. He *is* a picture of preverbal contentment. One day, someone in the building (it has to be an inside job—we have security, don't we?) spray-paints the baby. Silly protester. You have spray-painted reflective glass and a frame, not the baby inside.

David likes the Control Clerk because the Control Clerk is ambitious and reminds David of himself in his Control Clerk days, though he was never a Control Clerk per se. The Control Clerk likes David too, because David always tries to include him in whatever they're doing, whatever products are being sampled or stolen. That's not to say David and the Control Clerk have an uncomplicated relationship. They do. Whenever David feels his virility at issue, he takes it out on the Control Clerk. He makes the Control Clerk carry a nude mannequin with an erection up from the fifth floor to the tenth. He tries to sell a sixties-style buckskin jacket to the Control Clerk for two hundred dollars, exactly the Control Clerk's pay for a week. He has the Control Clerk send, via express mail at company expense, a copy of *Sports Illustrated* each week to a privileged friend in Apartheid-era South Africa. The friend sends David South African wine from the Stellenbosch region in return. The only time David ever gets angry at the Control Clerk is one week, when the *Sports Illustrated* doesn't get sent out. But the next week, all is forgiven. After work, he lets all the guys sample a bottle of Jägermeister, which the Control Clerk pretends not to loathe.

Ed, David's second-in-command, is the Jägermeister of the Modern Living Department. David is up on tenth in Editorial where Ed longs to be, while Ed has to languish next door to the Control Clerk's storehouse of an office because David is afraid if he moves Modern Living up to the tenth floor, the people in Editorial will steal all the things he wants to steal. Ed is from the East Coast and has a patrician, almost British accent, borrows the latest pod stereo system for his desk, and lines up bottles of cologne, his little fragrant paramilitary. El Jefe. Jägermeister. Master of the hunt. The *Playboy* para-male, eighties art of stylized martinis on his wall, jazz on the radio, the model of a Bentley on a shelf. He keeps tabs on the Control Clerk who is late and lazy and only wants to write and steal *Playboy* stationery and talk endlessly on the phone to his friends and use his franking privileges to send his short stories to magazines via personal messenger. David should see, David should fire the little twit of a Control Clerk, but he doesn't because it's the eighties!

All night long, all night, all night long, all night, all night long, all night.

The Control Clerk would like for Ed to like him, and he makes little forays. While passing his door, he sees Ed giggling. "What's so funny?" the Control Clerk asks.

Ed looks up from his desk, his face set grim. "Nothing," he stammers. "I was just thinking of something . . . to myself."

Did I just do that? the Control Clerk asks himself as he walks away. *Did I just poke my head into another person's office and demand to know what he was quietly laughing at?* The Control Clerk knows that older men sometimes have private thoughts, that their heads are maybe not so full of chatter as his, that as their lives are winding down, they start to contemplate more, think wistfully, play Sinatra, wear sweaters that fit too snugly. He just wishes he could get to know Ed a little better. Everything about Ed is just a best guess, because in a year and a half Ed has revealed exactly nothing about his life once he leaves 919 North Michigan Ave. The Control Clerk knows that David collects old movie posters and loves Sherlock Holmes. He's even been to David's home in Evanston and met his wife. And Jim, assistant editor of Modern Living, one year younger than the Control Clerk; he knows everything about Jim! He knows how hard-working Jim is, young wife and baby; Jim works two jobs. When he's done at *Playboy*, he works an evening shift at a furniture store in the suburbs.

The source of Ed's disdain must be this: with power comes privilege. If a Control Clerk has the same privileges as the editors of the department, then what glory remains for true modern livers? The Control Clerk shows up when he wants, hardly lifts a finger, resents wrapping packages and logging in bulls' penises, sees something wrong with sending *Sports Illustrated* at company expense to South Africa, doesn't seem to take his job seriously.

Ed knows this. He refuses to be mocked by a lowly Control Clerk. His office is the storeroom where all that is kept. It is the room in which small things matter terribly.

One day, they all leave the Control Clerk; all three of them fly off to the Mecca of Modern Livers, the Consumer Electronics Show in Las Vegas. No one will say exactly what went on. Nothing much, they say in that *heh heh* way that makes the Control Clerk know that a lot went on and it is his misfortune that that particular crew left him in dry dock this time. In the Control Clerk, envy rears, dreams of the Chicken Ranch.

But David makes up for it. They're working on a new story for the July issue, "The Toys of Summer." Into the Control Clerk's office streams a cavalcade of oversized toys: jet skis, a Harley, an Amazonian blow gun (this is David's stamp), portable mini-bar, a mountain bike, a James Bondian jet pack. In the final spread, young models wearing no purple splash on the jet ski, cloud walk in ultra-light bikinis, aim the blow gun at your heart, but none of these girls have ever been down here to Modern Living. Sometimes, the Control Clerk goes on excursions to find them, to bring them home. This is when he's asked by David to bring "product" to a photographer's studio for a shoot, sometimes on the twelfth floor, where all the stylists live, but more often to a private studio loft somewhere on the Gold Coast of Chicago. The girls are never there, just more *Playboy* Males posing as photographers wearing leather jackets or photo journalist vests. Screens and mirrors and sets suggest that the maiden is somewhere behind some door, but he never sees her. He just delivers product. Somehow, in 1983, dropping the article "the" makes the word "product" sound hipper, sexier. Whiffs of danger, drugs. Iran/Contra. As if it is all the same, all product, no need to distinguish.

He stays for a few minutes to see if he can catch a glimpse of the girls, but he never does, and then it's back in the cab to have the conversation:
The *Playboy* building? What do you do there?
I'm the masseuse. I rub down the bunnies.

One day, David shows up on the fifth floor and walks into the office. Ed and Jim are right behind him, Ed red-faced. "But David," he whines and then shuts up when he sees the Control Clerk on the floor, wrapping up the bull's penis walking stick to send home to its owner in Texas. A lot of these products are unsolicited. A lot of people make stupid useless things that have some vague scent of sex about them and think they're going to appear in the Modern Living section if they send their stuff. But a bull's penis is kind of a hard sell. It suggests—more than suggests, it *is*—emasculation, and hey, that's just not Modern Living. So David wants it sent back because no one likes it well enough to steal it.

"Hey," David says. "Why don't you come down to my office? We've got a photographer there who's going to shoot us for the Playbill section. It's for the 'Toys of Summer' spread."

The Control Clerk is about to say, "But I didn't have anything to do with that. I'm just a glorified shipping clerk." That's the term he's settled on these days. A glorified shipping clerk within editorial. Actually, there's nothing glorified about it, but it makes him feel better.

He doesn't get a chance to say it this time.

"But he didn't even work on the story," Ed blurts.

"Sure, I'd love to," the Control Clerk says.

And that's how he gets into *Playboy*, the magazine, how he becomes product. This picture is his bona fides, what gains him entrance. The image is small, just a bit bigger than a postage stamp, but he's there, with the others: David seated at his desk, a cigar in his hand, silver beard immaculately trimmed. Ed standing by his side, hand on David's shoulder, dressed in a sweater and slacks and round glasses. He looks like a dad at a little league game whose son has just hit one into the stands, a look that to this day the ex-Control Clerk can't fathom.

It's just a jet ski, damn it.

Jim stands, also sweater clad on the other side of David. Ever since Las Vegas, he's had this hey-baby-I'm-no-ordinary-manager-of-a-furniture-outlet look, and he's turning it on here. But he's twenty-three and he has hair. He can be forgiven. Leaning on his shoulder, standing in the back, is the Control Clerk, arm draped on Jim's shoulder, hand dangling over David's head as though holding a sprig of mistletoe. He's an emaciated lad, no one you'd ever worry about in a dark alley. He has the biggest smile of the bunch, the only one that shows teeth. Are *Playboy* Males supposed to show their teeth? Apparently not. What seductiveness lies in a full-toothed grin?

When he first joined the *Playboy* team, the Control Clerk was given a key to the Chicago *Playboy* Club by the HR Manager, Carol Divine. (Not to suggest she lacked credentials, but with a name like that, what self-disrespecting men's magazine wouldn't hire her for HR?) The *Playboy* Club went out of business ten days later. It then became just another unremarkable building in Lincoln Park. The idea of *Playboy* fled its smoky walls as soon as it closed its doors, the way that all buildings eventually lose the ideas they try to contain. This is the mortality of an idea, how it becomes a ghost wandering the windy streets in search of a soul or a place to rest. It's amazing how quickly a building learns new ideas. The *Playboy* building wasn't always the *Playboy* building. First, it was the Palmolive building. It was where the idea of soap lived and the babies on its walls didn't masturbate, except when the guards went home and the lights went out. On its roof were klieg lights that used to shine into the cloudy horizon of Lake Michigan, blinking out *soap soap soap* to all those grimy Great Lake sailors who longed for a little freshness. But then it became *Playboy* and the klieg lights went out because no one needed to advertise its location because it lives in us all and the neighbors complained that the klieg lights shone into their windows a harshness they could not tolerate. And then the Great *Playboy* Spirit left the *Playboy* building and moved away and Modern Living was modern no longer.

One evening, he meets Sandy at Crosscurrents, an upscale bar near his apartment. She works there sometimes and the Control Clerk's roommate, who also works there, introduces them. Turns out she's an ex-*Playboy* bunny. She used to work the Chicago club. She's in her early thirties and has a kid, or maybe a couple, but she looks his age and she's . . . . what's the term they're using in the early eighties? She's a babe. She's hot. She's a fox. Not that he'd ever use those terms. He hates those terms. He hates all terms. But the feelings those terms communicate are another matter. He wears those feelings like Michael Jackson's glove. He's a moonwalk away from heaven, and he and Sandy go back to his apartment and talk for exactly twelve and a half minutes before they head for the bedroom and all he thinks of is her hotness.

He fondles her fevered breasts and she moans, "Oh, Control Clerk! You feel so *good*, Control Clerk!" He'd like to see Sandy again, but his old girlfriend calls the next day and wants to get back together with him. His roommate, five years older and much more experienced, answers the next time Sandy calls. He handles it for him like his own personal sexual valet. "No, I'm sorry," he says with a smile like a bastard everyone secretly admires. "He won't be seeing you again." If she were a glossy page, she'd be flipped.

When the Control Clerk finally quits *Playboy*, he travels only about a mile to the Art Institute of Chicago, where he will start teaching as an adjunct. His going-away lunch, at the Cliff Dwellers Club, across the street from the Art Institute, is attended only by Jim and David. Ed boycotts it, which kind of stuns the Control Clerk, the depth of Ed's hatred for him. Ed feels personally affronted by the Control Clerk. Perhaps it's simply cultural, tribal, the Control Clerk thinks, many years distant. The Control Clerk, stinking with unschooled desire. Ed, cologned and private. Oh well. David and Jim at least harbor no ill will. They know that this wasn't the right job for him anyway. In his place, they've promoted, sort of, at Carol Divine's suggestion, an unutterably happy mail clerk, the first African American in Editorial, who will not complain about sending *Sports Illustrated* to South Africa, and who, David seems to think, will be satisfied to retire in fifty years as a Control Clerk with fifty signed commendations from an eternally youthful Hef. After three martinis, David says, "Promise to shoot me if I ever get old," and the Control Clerk promises to shoot him, and then they shake hands all around and stagger off and the Control Clerk will never set foot in *Playboy* again or see David grow old, or remember any of them except in occasional dreams and in that odd photo, uncovered during one of his many moves, that was snapped to commemorate the "Toys of Summer."

Eventually, he moves away from Chicago, but returns in 1986 to give a reading at the School of the Art Institute of his writings, the ones he wrote on the job at *Playboy*. And where do they put him up but the deserted *Playboy* Mansion? Yes, Hef has donated the mansion to the School of the Art Institute to use as dorms, and they put the Control Clerk and his girlfriend up in the room that was Hef's own bedroom: leather furniture, a round bed, mirrors on the ceiling, of course, a broken telephone in the bathroom. The idea of this building has not yet fled. The idea of longing has been bottled up all these years in this bedroom with all those drunken men who can't leave either. It's a waif now, sad and wide-eyed and nearly skeletal.

At some level, he remains the Control Clerk. He will always be the Control Clerk. As he grows older, he will perform a little Control Clerk Eucharist—*I am the body and I am only the body over which I have no control*—whenever he feels small and out of place, whenever he pretends he's someone he's not, whenever he puts the word "glorified" in front of anything he does.

A Word from Our Sponsors

After the sound thrashing it received at its last match-up, "Art for Art's Sake" has demanded a rematch with the reigning world champion, "Making a Buck or Two." Postponed and rescheduled after the unfortunate incident in which "Making a Buck or Two" bit off and spit out the ear of "Art for Art's Sake," we are glad to report that the two gladiators are once again fit and eager to pound one another to smithereens. Ladies and gentlemen. . . .

Provincetown: Fame, What's Your Name? What's Your Name?

The Smithsonian Archives of American Art contains an interview done in 1963 with the art dealer Richard Bellamy, in which Bellamy speaks briefly of my father, Cecil Hemley. For that reason alone, the interview interests me. I imagine that most people reading this will not have heard of Richard Bellamy, much as they will have little idea who Cecil Hemley was. The interviewer, identified only as "Baker," has even less name recognition. Perhaps Baker was a giant of the art world, but I'll leave that for one of his progeny or many (I'm certain) admirers to reveal. We can't know who everyone is. Bellamy, the director of the Green Gallery, comes across in the interview as a little crabby, forgetful, eccentric, perhaps a bit loopy. I imagine Baker, an artist himself who studied just a few years earlier with the legendary Hans Hoffman in Provincetown, furtively glancing at the reel-to-reel machine every now and again to make sure it's functioning. They're apparently old friends or at least acquaintances Baker is younger, full of self-confidence and opinions of the art world, a little annoying with his excited interruptions. His goal, for the moment, is to get a clear picture from Bellamy of the explosive New York art scene of the late 1940s, '50s, and '60s, and his own role in it as an art dealer.

RB: [A] very important exhibit took place in the summer of 1949 in Provincetown. I don't know who arranged it, I can't even quite remember the story, but in the summer of 1949, there was a very large exhibit, let's say fifty artists had a show in Provincetown. The sitter at that gallery . . . was an author. His name is Cecil Hemley, he's a poet and he's just finished a novel . . .

B: Hemory?

RB: Cecil Hemley. He's a describable person I believe and probably a nice minor poet. But at any rate he was sitting there and I heard him make comments about certain, well, okay, then I'll come later and say who was there, represented there was practically everybody on the avant garde New York scene except deKooning who did not submit a picture. Pollock was there with a very great picture, I remember it very well, I think the title was *number 17*, Hofmann, Baziotes, not sure whether David Smith had a painting there or not, Tworkov, Fritz Bultman, Marca Relli, you know, etc. Perhaps Rothko, I'm not sure, I think so, and Stamos. I remember this poet, Cecil Hemley, saying to somebody in talking about the pictures, well you know, I just don't see how art can do without the lyrical. Now look at this beautiful tiny little painting of Stamos and look at that Pollock, now how can you get away with something like that? I do remember this and I remember some other statements he made, but it's not a Cecil Hemley day. But it was a very important exhibition. I think probably important because I don't think that there was any group exhibition of its size that had ever been assembled before, except I guess the Eighth Street show, which was, when was the Eighth Street show before? Well it was just about the same time, probably a little bit later, maybe. At any rate, what was I saying, what was I talking about?

A Describable Person

Indeed, Cecil Hemley was "a describable person," whatever that means, though I love the phrase. In 1949, Cecil Hemley lived in Provincetown, Massachusetts. He'd grown up in Manhattan, had attended Amherst at the age of fourteen, and later the University of Chicago and Yale Drama School. Early on, his path was that of the artist who disdained money, perhaps in part because he'd grown up with so much of it around. His father, a well-to-do lawyer who lived in the Essex hotel, groomed his sons for the family business, and my father's brothers not only retained the family wealth but passed it along to their children, a statement that cannot be made about my father's children.

Undoubtedly, my father's spendthrift ways can be traced to doting parents. At the outbreak of World War II, my grandfather pulled some strings and had my father stationed first at Camp Crowder, Missouri (which he hated), and later to Provincetown, Massachusetts (which he loved), of all places. Perhaps my grandfather thought he was doing my father a favor, but when he found out, the story goes, my father demanded to be sent overseas, and he was. Before he was shipped off, he married a local girl named Katherine. He was sent to Pearl Harbor on the day the atomic bomb was dropped on Hiroshima, and he spent the rest of the war writing *The History of Censorship in the Middle Pacific*. His commanding officer, Lieutenant Colonel John D. Knappenberger, gave him his first good review when he was transferred to another post: "He was assiduous in the collection of the material and his writing and editing were superior, changing a mass of unrelated facts into an interesting and readable narrative. The efficient, energetic and intelligent manner in which he carried out his assignment is a credit to Lieutenant Hemley."

No one cares much these days about *The History of Censorship in the Middle Pacific* (Amazon.com Sales Rank: N/A), if they ever did, though there's something catchy about the title. Such books, of course, were written for neither art's sake nor money, but for duty. Still, it pleases me to know that my father tackled this project with the same generosity and esprit that was his hallmark later in life.

Upon his discharge, my father made his way back to Provincetown to join Katherine, whose father, happily for my father, owned an art gallery.

In Hebrew, there's a phrase, Dayanu, which means, "It would be enough." At Passover, Jews sing a song "Dai Dayanu," extolling God's generosity. If God had done this for the Jews, the song goes, Dayanu. If God had done that, Dayanu. I'm certainly not comparing my father to God. After all, my father is a Describable Person and God, most certainly, is not. But if my father's only mark upon the world of arts and letters had been this gallery, Dayanu.

Bellamy had it wrong. My father was more than the gallery sitter; he was the owner of the gallery (or at least its manager through his father-in-law) and more importantly, co-organizer of the show, known as Forum 49. This show was arguably the most important show of its time. The young avant-garde of New York had been frozen out of the gallery scene, and my father and the poet Weldon Kees decided to hold a summer-long series of lectures about the artists and their work, starting big with the topic, "What is art?" With this groundbreaking art displayed in the gallery, they brought together fifty of the artists who, after this show, became giants of the art world. The show featured Robert Motherwell, Jackson Pollock, Mark Rothko, Fritz Bultman, Adolph Gottlieb, and a host of others. It was the largest show of abstract expressionism to date, and as much as anything else of its time, it revolutionized the art world. The moment was ripe for the show as, at the end of the summer, *Life* magazine did a four-page spread on Pollock, and asked the question, "Is he the greatest living painter in the United States?"

It's odd, I think, that Bellamy would remember my father bemoaning the loss of the lyrical in art. At least this seems odd out of context. It's true that my father celebrated the lyric, the personal expression of the artist, but he undoubtedly appreciated the abstract and theoretical as well. Not only was he one of the organizers of Forum 49, but his first cousin, Adolph Gottlieb, was one of the featured artists. I think he was simply expressing his understanding that ultimately the personal and "classic" would be appreciated again, and that the abstract expressionists would simply become part of the continuum of human artistic expression. But indeed, it was the lyric that spoke to my father most deeply—his own poetry was classically oriented, full of Greek allusions, and to this day, the Poetry Society of America gives the Cecil Hemley Award for the best lyric poem, an award that several of my friends and colleagues have won.

But when one mentions Forum 49, it's Weldon Kees who is brought up as one of the driving forces, not my father. I think this is because Kees is a more recognizable name, nothing else. I certainly don't begrudge him the stature of his poetry, which I must admit, I largely prefer to my father's, though it pains me to say this. But because of this, my father has been relegated to the role of a gallery sitter, a minor poet minding the fort for the famous, whining about the loss of the lyrical in art.

A Poetic Interlude: A Word from Our Sponsors

Both my parents knew Weldon Kees. Actually, my mother knew Kees before my father did, when she was stationed in Denver during the war, teaching photography to GIs. My mother, Elaine Gottlieb (no relation to Adolph Gottlieb), knew Kees when he was a public librarian in Denver, had dinner with him and his wife several times, and remembered him as a "pleasant" man. My father's association with Kees came later, as did his association with my mother, which produced two lyrics, namely my brother and myself.

Kees and my father were probably two of a kind—both Renaissance men to a certain degree (not only was Kees a poet and an art lover, but he was also a jazz enthusiast). Like most modernists, Weldon Kees munched on despair like breakfast cereal, but despair in the modernist view wasn't personal so much as a despair for the world as a whole. Still, the modernists killed themselves in droves, including Weldon Kees who allegedly jumped off the Golden Gate Bridge in 1955. The lack of a corpse only added to his mystique, judging by the many rumors of him living a secret life in Mexico, born again, as it were, unheralded but happy and free from the scourge of modernism.

A Cecil Hemley Day

My father returned to New York after his marriage to Katherine ended. There, he and Arthur Cohen founded the Noonday Press. Cohen, young and passionate about literature, had the money, and my father had the experience and literary know-how. His own family money was long gone. In the 1950s, Noonday published the best writers of its day from around the world: Boris Pasternak, Herman Hesse, Jean Paul Sartre, Louise Bogan (Hosanna!

He actually published poetry) Machado de Assis, the philosopher Karl Jaspers. As Noonday was an independent press, whatever my father wanted to publish, he published.

My father had since met and married my mother, then a well-known short story writer, and one evening in 1953, they visited their friends, the Talbots, owners of the New Yorker Theater. After dinner, Dan Talbot read to them a story in the May issue of the *Partisan Review*. The story, "Gimpel the Fool," was by a middle-aged Jewish émigré named Isaac Singer, written in Yiddish, and translated by Saul Bellow. My parents were "wild" for the story, and my father was determined to meet this writer. My father's timing was impeccable. Singer had previously published one book, *The Family Moskat*, with Knopf, but he had been terribly unhappy with the cuts forced upon him by Alfred Knopf. He had been required to cut the entire middle of the novel because Knopf felt the book was too long. Singer consented but felt bitterly that his book had lost a sense of itself.

And so my father "acquired" Singer. Yet it didn't seem like an acquisition so much as the happy meeting of two people who were passionate for literature. I can't say that my father knew how big Singer would become; in some ways, he probably didn't care. That's not to say he lacked ambition. On the contrary, his ambitions were always larger than simple monetary gain. He had helped stage Forum 49 because he thought the under-recognized artists represented in the show deserved the world's attention. He undoubtedly felt the same about Singer, who also didn't lack ambition either. What Singer needed was someone who believed in his work, and he needed a co-translator. Singer's English was good enough to hold his own in a conversation, but not good enough to write polished English. Singer not only needed a publisher; he needed a writer.

From that point on, my father became his editor and both of my parents translated his work. Singer was prolific and needed other translators as well, but my father was Singer's preferred co-translator. At least as important, the two of them became the closest of friends.

One might step back a moment and look at Singer's choice to leave Knopf and go to Noonday. Even in the 1950s, such a move probably didn't make monetary sense. It would be the equivalent now of a writer leaving Knopf to go to, say, Graywolf, one of the bigger independent publishers today. The assumption now would be that an author who went from Knopf to an independent press had to make this step (down) because he or she lacked sales at the larger house. No one would assume that an author, given a choice, would choose an independent press over a large one.

1957 New York State Income Tax Return: Cecil and Elaine Hemley

A little over a month before I was born in 1958, my parents filed their tax form (yes, it's bizarre that I actually have this document, but I come from a family that is loath to throw out any piece of paper with writing on it). My parents, at the time, lived in Riverdale, the Bronx. My father listed his profession as publisher/writer. My mother listed her profession as writer. Their combined gross income for 1957 was $5,343.61. Even in 1957, this was not a lot of money. In inflation-adjusted dollars, this would be a little over $58,000 today. No one was getting rich.

And that's in part why Noonday was sold to Farrar, Straus. Singer wasn't a household name, but he was seen as an important writer, and Roger Straus wanted him as well as the rest of Noonday's incredible list. After the sale, the only editor Roger Straus brought over to Farrar, Straus was my father, the visionary and exceedingly hard worker (remember Lieutenant Hemley working on his *History of Censorship in the Middle Pacific*) who was in many ways indispensable. At Farrar, Straus, he continued to nurture writers. Sure, he made some mistakes. My mother once told me he passed on Joseph Heller's *Catch-22*. Ouch. But what editor doesn't make mistakes? Susan Sontag, then a young nothing of a writer, was so shy, she simply knocked on my father's door, left her manuscript at the threshold, and fled before he answered. It didn't matter. He saw her talent immediately and he championed her to a skeptical Robert Giroux, who "doubted the commercial value of Sontag's work," according to FSG historian Boris Kachka. But the pressures on my father, now in his late forties, had begun to tell. A chain smoker and overweight, he suffered from hypertension. In some respects, his love of literature was literally killing him, and so in 1963, he quit Farrar, Straus, and accepted a job as director of the Ohio University Press and lecturer in the English Department. Athens was his haven, a place where he thought he'd be able to concentrate on his own writing and the latest Singer translation without the distractions and pressures of New

York. In August 1963, Singer wrote to my father—their mutual devotion is obvious in his letter:

> Dear Cecil.
>
> When your letter reached Miami I had left and this is the reason I am late in answering you. In Miami I didn't feel it so much but here in N.Y., I am missing you, missing your call in the morning. You somehow always managed to convey to me some good news. Now, nothing happens. However, I am working hard on *The Manor*. There is much to do. Naturally, I will consult you at the end. I will do nothing without your advice and consent. I hope you will visit our old rotten city. From your letter it is difficult to judge how you feel in your new place. The trouble with all these paradises is that they become soon boring, but I am sure that you will be able to do a lot of work and with more peace of mind than here, and for a writer that is the main thing . . . .
>
> I hope that your being there and I here will not spoil our friendship. As far as I'm concerned, I am devoted to you as ever and I hope it will be mutual. Please give my best regards to Elaine, Nola and the little ones . . .
>
> Your devoted co-translator
>
> Isaac

The pressures on my father had little to do with his physical locale. *The Manor* was a long novel and it was difficult for him to find time to work on the translation, given his teaching, his work at the OU Press, his work on his own novel, and the normal pressures of family life. In September 1964, Roger Straus wrote him a chiding letter. In the letter, Straus mentioned that they were publishing a whole cavalcade of Singer material: a new collection of stories titled *Short Friday* and reissuing *The Family Moskat* under the Farrar, Straus imprint. It made Straus unhappy that *The Manor* had not yet been delivered. As a publisher, he said, one could "smell the moment juste" and it was slipping away. In the past six months, they had succeeded in placing Singer stories in such national magazines as *The Saturday Evening Post* and *Harpers*. He wanted *The Manor* to come out no later than August or early September 1965. The book, he asserted, had book club possibilities as well as first serial possibilities, and they needed time to "exploit" them. He ended the letter by telling my father he needed the manuscript by no later than January 1965. "Can you guarantee it?" he demanded.

The letter only made my father more frantic, and he wrote to Singer in despair over it. My father wasn't interested in the moment juste. He was interested in the work. He was an idealist, not a good businessman, that much was clear. Singer, as always, tried to comfort him. He was on my father's side and would do his best to smooth things over with Roger.

There was good reason for Singer's faith in my father. My father was a poet and a craftsman, and he approached the translation as a calling, not as a business venture. Singer knew this. My father's masterpiece of translation was Singer's *The Slave*, arguably Singer's masterpiece too. When Singer was awarded the Nobel Prize for Literature, *The Slave* was given special mention, and I'm certain Singer never would have made it to Sweden without my father's help on all levels, as a friend, as an editor, and as a co-translator.

Of *The Manor*, only this can be said. My father, feeling such pressure, could not complete it. I'm not sure how far he got in the translation, but obviously not far enough. *The Manor* did not appear until 1967, long after the moment juste of which Roger Straus spoke. Singer's nephew Joseph had to finish the translation. This is a book not often praised. One reviewer spoke of its relentlessly short, declarative sentences. Whether this was Singer's fault or his nephew's, I can't say for sure. But it wasn't my father's. In 1966, my father died of a massive heart attack.

My father told my older brother Jonathan in 1965 that he had been offered a job in Chicago for $50,000 a year, but he wasn't going to take it because he wanted more time to work on his own novel. "Don't tell your mother," he urged my brother. In today's dollars, he'd been offered an incredible $496,000. That amount of money took our breaths away when my brother and I discussed it on the phone, my brother having just calculated the adjusted amount. "He should have taken it," Jonathan said, though with no bitterness in his voice. "But he only lived another year anyway. Maybe they would have given him a life insurance policy at least."

The History of Censorship in Middle America

Some years ago, I ran across some reviews of *The Known World* by Edward P. Jones, a bestseller at the time: a largely positive but mixed review from *Pub-*

lishers Weekly followed by several other positive reviews and many glowing reviews by various readers of the book. Then I came to a review by another author, Hugh Pearson. The title of the review was: "A Good Concept But the Raise is Troubling."

The Raise? I wondered. *What does he mean by "the Raise"?* I read on. The review itself was troubling. Mr. Pearson began the review evenly enough, but soon lost his footing after he revealed that Edward P. Jones and he had once shared the same literary agent. What bothered Mr. Pearson, he claimed, was the fact that this book portraying a relationship between a white man and an African American woman had been "excessively praised." He went on to complain that Jonathan Yardley, writing in the *Washington Post*, had praised Edward P. Jones for traveling back and forth in time in his narrative, but had had the audacity to criticize Hugh Pearson's own book *Under the Knife: How a Wealthy Negro Surgeon Wielded Power in the Jim Crow South* for using the same technique! Yardley, he claimed, had written the one and only negative review of his book, and that just shows how "POLITICAL" reviewing is.

No, Mr. Pearson, there was no conspiracy out to get you. Nor me. The publishing world has always been driven by numbers—just not as obviously as now. Even in the 1950s, editors who believed in "Art for Art's Sake," like my father, either burned out or eventually died, everything in life, even literature, being finally Darwinian.

Literature and our participation in art's continuum have simply become more efficient and democratic than in days gone by.

For decades, malcontents and doomsayers have been heralding the end of literature as we know it. Happily, we can report that this is far from the case! More books are published every year than they were twenty or thirty years ago. Of course, books that aren't successful go out of print faster than they did thirty or forty years ago, but apparently these are only the books of malcontents and doomsayers. If their books were worth anything, they would have sold to a grateful reading public.

In 1962, Curtis Zahn wrote in *Trace*, an influential literary magazine then, a short essay titled "Towards Print (Are Littlemags Our Final Voice?)." The tone of it is a little smug and snooty, but all the same, he raises some interesting points, the main point being that authors increasingly practice self-censorship because of market concerns. The literary magazine, he sees as the last bastion of "public truth" (one could still utter the word "truth" in 1962 without blushing). Radio, television, the press, and the "slicks" are all damned, in his opinion, by the relentless pursuit of profit. He writes:

The American publisher is concerned more with money than morals. If readers subscribe, if the audience watches, if the consumer buys, then the stockholders get their 9 percent. And the writer (having been bought) is paid.

By now, it's not a new argument, and the culprits are all too familiar. Ho hum. Tell us something new, Curtis. At least something entertaining. But he refuses and ends on a predictably whiny and self-important note:

But will they [the literary magazines] get past the voluntary censorship imposed by the U.S. reader, suckled on a saccharine formula of sweet slops (with rib tickles), before it is too late? I cannot say what can be done; I am only able to say what must be done.

I'm not sure what a sweet slop is, but I'm sure I'd like it (rib tickles, I've never been able to fully appreciate).

A Poetic Interlude: The Sweet Slops (with Rib Tickles)
of Milo the Incontinent Dachshund

Several years ago, I submitted a poem to the most democratic and efficient publisher in the world, The National Library of Poetry, in Owen Mills, Maryland. This outfit understands that there are many more people in the country who write poetry than actually read it, and so they accept virtually every poem that comes their way, proclaiming its genius and originality, and then publishing it in a thick volume with hundreds of other brilliant and original poems. Then they sell the volumes to the contributors for seventy-five dollars a pop. Understandably, most of the contributors buy the volume.

So I decided to channel my incontinent Dachshund Milo and write a poem from his point of view, not hiding the fact that the poem was written by a dog. I wondered if they'd publish it.

A Million Bambis
A million Bambis crowd the hillside
Not celluloid, but fur and flesh

They tremble in the 'dozers' shadow
The steady hum
Of cars below
Crushing a thousand Thumpers
In the mad dash to the mall.
A million Bambis:
No voice, only tears
No food, they're just deer.
No vote, only a mote
In harsh humanity's eye.
No happy ending, just Progress–
Relentless, repetitive
Like a theme park ride.

—Milo Hemley

This seemed to me to capture Milo's empathetic, compassionate, and despairing soul. Sure enough, within a week or so, I received word that Milo's poem deserved a special place in the latest volume of the National Library of Poetry, *Etches in Time*. If I wanted to purchase a short bio note, I was informed it would cost an additional twenty-five dollars. I happily paid the fee, figuring this was a small price to pay for such exposure. On the form I filled out, I wrote that Milo was a miniature Dachshund. Under clubs, I wrote "American Kennel Club." Children: Unknown. Philosophy: "The Place where you pee is where you are." Next, I paid an additional thirty-five dollars to have Milo's poem recorded by a professional actor and another forty dollars to have Milo's poem immortalized on a plaque. I wondered how many Milo-inspired products the National Library of Poetry could sell me. The options seemed endless, and I only stopped because I could no longer afford to immortalize Milo. I did not purchase the laminated playing-card size copies of Milo's poem, nor did I purchase the website for three hundred dollars, though I was sorely tempted to see Milo's big schnoz and his drooly tongue on his very own website.

But my biggest disappointment was that those canny editors at the National Library of Poetry did not publish Milo's biography as I had written it. Instead, they published the biography belonging to one Thomas H. Johnson Jr. of Nashville, Tennessee, whose philosophy had nothing to do with pee, but rather was summed up as "I write from the heart with an open mind." Obviously, publishing Milo's bio as I had written it might have freaked out his neighbors on the page. "Emily, what's a dog doing in here? They say this dog wrote this Bambi poem!"

I think the editors' worries were unwarranted. I doubt anyone in *Etches in Time* gave a glance at anyone else's bio but his or her own. I know Milo didn't.

The Language That Can Comfort Guinea Pigs

In an intriguing piece titled "The Art of Suicide," A. Alverez, writing in 1970 in the *Partisan Review*, noted that quite a few modern writers and artists had killed themselves: Virginia Woolf, Cesare Pavese, Paul Celan, Randall Jarrell, Sylvia Plath, Hemingway, Mayakovsky, Yesenin, Tsvetayeva, Modigliani, Arshile Gorky, Mark Gertler, and Mark Rothko. Of course, there were plenty of fine artists and writers who hadn't killed themselves, but even so, Alverez posited that in the last sixty or so years, "the casualty rate among the gifted seems out of all proportion." Alverez saw this in part as a result of the radical experimentation among artists and writers of the twentieth century. Alverez writes:

> But for the more serious artists experiment has not been a matter of merely tinkering with the machinery. Instead, it has provided a context in which he explores the perennial question, "What am I?" without benefit of moral, cultural or even technical securities. Since part of his gift is also a weird knack of sensing and expressing the strains of his time in advance of other people, the movement of the modern arts has been, with continual minor diversions, toward a progressively more intolerable sense of disaster. It is as though, by taking to its limits Conrad's dictum "In the destructive element immerse," his whole role in society has changed; instead of being a Romantic hero and liberator, he has become a victim, a scapegoat.

Twentieth-century art was all about forging "a language which will somehow absolve or validate absurd death, and to accept the existential risks involved in doing so. . . . 'There are no words in any human language,' wrote a Hiroshima survivor, 'which can comfort guinea pigs who do not know the cause of their death.'"

We're beyond death and its causes now. We're on to sequels. *Hiroshima 2*? The sequel is familiar and comfortable because the past becomes as safe and pliable a haven as the future is (still) uncertain and grim. Nothing has changed in that respect. If I sound nostalgic for modernism, that's not my aim. What I mean to say is that success in the ways we have come to define it might ultimately get in the way of more important matters and greater talents.

The Godfather

If I had been a better son, if I had been the hero in a Shakespearean tragedy, if I had been a Romantic, I might have tried to do something to avenge my father's death. But truthfully, the thought never even entered my mind. When I was ushered in to meet the octogenarian Roger Straus, he seemed like the Godfather to me, all-powerful and all-knowing. Farrar, Straus and Giroux had bought my latest book, and I was there at FSG's offices in Union Square turning in my manuscript to my editor. Before I left, he told me, "Come, I'm sure Roger would like to see you." Even without considering myself Hamlet, I still thought it was an odd moment, meeting Roger Straus for the first time in my adult life. Straus, that old publishing battle-ax, the last of his kind, still came to the office every day. Frankly, I don't remember much of my audience with Straus. His secretary of over forty years reminisced a little about my father. Straus's references were, not surprisingly, all about books. Mostly, I remember him grousing about the books of various authors, all of which he pronounced "bad" or "very bad." I felt in some ways that I'd come home, much as I felt in my early twenties when I had a seven-month fellowship at the Fine Arts Work Center in Provincetown, and met various friends of my father's, as well as my half brother and half sister, for the first time since my father's funeral. My father's call was quite powerful to me always, and in some ways I have mapped my life around his. This happens naturally, I think, when one loses a parent at an early age.

For years, Noonday had been a paperback line of Farrar, Straus and Giroux, and I held out hope that perhaps Noonday would publish the paperback edition of my book. In this way I could pay homage to my father. But alas, Noonday was slowly being phased out of existence, and by the time my book was finally finished, the imprint was gone entirely. Nothing now remained, tangibly at least, of my father's legacy. Except, perhaps, for me.

When I was born, Singer visited my mother and me in the hospital and pronounced that I would grow up to be "half poet and half publisher," a prediction we always took seriously in my family. To me, the two were inseparable. Could one be a publisher without also being a poet? Could one be a poet without being a publisher also? According to my editor, when my book was being presented at a marketing meeting, Roger spoke up: "Listen," he said, "I want everyone to know he's part of the family." Exactly like the Godfather.

But before that, long before that, I sat in the waiting room of Farrar, Straus and Giroux, ready to deliver my book, humbled by the walls plastered with the many honors FSG's authors have received. Twenty-one of its authors had received the Nobel Prize, more than any other publisher in the world. I felt the way I always feel in the offices of a publishing house, or among writers who care as much about the voices of other writers as they care about their own: as though I've stepped into a place that's safe, a haven, a paradise beyond death, despair, or dollars, into the antechambers of the temple where my family has always worshipped.

The Unmentionable One

Mario Praz, Of Curses and Beauty, *Noonday Press, $28, pp. 277*

Every person I've known in my life, and I'd venture to include as well, all those on earth I have not been acquainted with, carry with them a curse. My good fortune is in having known from an early age, the manifestation if not the exact reasons for my curse. The vast assemblage of humanity, by contrast, know very little of their own particular curses and spend the better part of their lives attempting to untangle curse from blessing, much like the unfortunate protagonist of James' "The Beast in the Jungle," the curse in his case being that he let his life slip by unacted upon.

So might begin this curious and ultimately moving memoir by the Italian art historian and literary critic Mario Praz. An unvarnished and overt memoir would have been painful and/or too mundane for him to write, as he had previously written one of the most eccentric memoirs ever written, *The House of Life*, a memoir told through the possessions with which he filled his apartment in Rome. But if he had been coaxed to write another memoir, perhaps he would have found a little fascination with the attitude of others toward him, that nearly everyone in Italian society considered him *portava iella*, a jinx. Known by some as "L'Anglista," for his vast knowledge of English literature, he was most famous in academic circles worldwide for his 1933 groundbreaking study of Romanticism, *The Romantic Agony*, and for his exquisite sense of interior design, as demonstrated in his work *An Illustrated History of Interior Decoration from Pompeii to Art Nouveau.*

But in Rome, among friends, foes, and acquaintances, he was known as "L'Innominabile" "the Unmentionable," an irredeemable carrier of misfortune whose presence always brought some measure of disaster. When Maria Callas lost her voice during a performance at the Teatro dell'Opera of Bellini's *Norma*, she found grim satisfaction upon learning that Professor Praz had been in the audience. If he approached an acquaintance at a restaurant or café, as he did once the famous Zambrano sisters, Maria and Ariceli, they'd cower quietly, in direct opposition to their vibrant natures, until he moved on.

How much did this perception weigh on him: otherwise sane and intelligent people certain he carried evil with him, all because of a congenital limp (a sure sign of the devil)? How did the almost gothic fascination others had with accursedness determine his scholarly fascination with the Romantics whom he blasted as immoral and decadent in their obsessions with beauty and horror? Or conversely, his own appreciation of beautiful exteriors? Beginning his *Romantic Agony* with a chapter on Medusa, how much did he see himself reflected in her, his own ability to alter the life of anyone in his presence? An anxiety with no possibility of escape is the main theme of the Gothic tales, he wrote. Describing these anxieties and resisting them was in some fashion his life's work. In surrounding himself with beautiful objects that carried memories of his life for him, he created one memoir. In writing about the Romantics and their free-floating anxieties that sought expression in the supernatural, he wrote in a sense another "covert autobiography" (as John Russell called *The House of Life* in an article in the *New York Times* shortly after Praz's death in 1982).

The missing fork of this trident of memoirs is the one he might have written perhaps titled *The Anxiety Catcher* or *The Unmentionable: A Memoir* or *Of Curses and Beauty*.

Let's say this curious book exists, though only in manuscript form, typed a year before Praz's death. If you go looking for this book you might or might not find it, but you will certainly find him, or at least one branch of his autobiography at the Mario Praz Museum brimming with the furnishings and books that soothed his restless and often lonely existence. Perhaps hidden in a secret compartment of a burnished cherrywood desk with ebony accents on the third floor of the Palazzo Primoli, *Of Curses and Beauty* is kept, admired and reread by the museum's docents, but otherwise kept under wraps, the true nature of Mario Praz jealously guarded. While we are unable at this juncture to properly review it, we eagerly await its manifestation, discovery, and eventual publication.

PART 2

Ghosts I Follow

How to Change History

Every family has its casualties, and Roy was ours. My mother's first cousin, the son of my great-aunt Gus, was a legend. His glorious moment came during the Japanese attack on Pearl Harbor. For years I told people that Roy was one of seven survivors of the USS *Arizona*. Actually, three hundred and thirty-four men survived the bombing of the *Arizona*. In my mind, that famous image of the ship blowing up melded with the story of Roy. But who knows? Maybe I didn't invent this. Perhaps he *was* on the *Arizona* on that day, even though he was in the Army, not the Navy. He was based at nearby Fort Weaver, and the men from that base sometimes worked on the ships. How else to explain another indispensable nugget of family lore whenever Roy was mentioned: Roy swam in the fiery waters of Pearl Harbor for three hours. There's no way to know all the details for certain as he's long dead and his service records have disappeared.

This was his calling card in my family: Roy, Survivor of Pearl Harbor. I'm not trying to make light of that because his is not a funny story, but it was a fact on a flashcard, something to be memorized and recognized whenever I saw him, which was not frequently because he lived in New Jersey with his family. My family was always moving around the Midwest, and we only came together in the summers, at my grandmother's beach house. *He swam around Pearl Harbor for three hours! He had to swim underwater.* Roy swam and swam. I envisioned him almost fishlike, diving deeper as dead men bobbed and sank around him. When he emerged, he was changed forever, of course, but not like America: cleansed by its blood sacrifice, reenergized, mighty in its resolve. He spent the next year in a psychiatric ward in Denver, recovering from deep but invisible wounds. From the hospital, he sent photos of himself pre-Pearl: his face open and sweet. This was the face he sent to friends and relatives: Roy in pith helmet, smiling in hidden anguish.

My mother, whose war job was to teach photography to the Army Air Corps in Denver, visited him in the hospital there and remembers him as charming and funny. When he returned home, his father was willing to do anything for him. Roy enrolled in the Academy of Dramatic Art. He built toy furniture. He took up photography. But he was too "scatterbrained" (the word my mother used) to be involved in anything for very long. Now we'd recognize it as PTSD. His father, my great-uncle Rob, was wealthy from the manufacture of leather desk sets. Roy, always smiling, saw himself as an entertainer and lived off his father and stayed for a time with my great-grandmother in her large house in Brooklyn. One day, he burned the bed in his room and narrowly avoided setting the whole house on fire. Much later, he nearly set his car on fire when a cigarette he threw away blew back into the car. I mention this because no details are innocent, are they? I see his whole life after Pearl Harbor as ringed by fiery waters that he himself set ablaze, trying to dive underneath.

As a child, the last thing you want in your adults is hidden depths and aftermaths. Ships blowing up are fine as long as your adult can walk away coolly as fireballs erupt behind him. I simply knew him as a good joke teller. One joke in particular was so unremarkable and corny that I should have forgotten it. And it's the only joke I have ever been able to commit to memory.

It goes like this:

A woman is sitting in her home alone one evening when the phone rings. "Hello? Who is it?"

"I am the Viper, and I'm three blocks away." The line goes dead, and the woman thinks, *Must be a wrong number.*

The phone rings again. She doesn't pick it up at first, but it keeps ringing. She could unplug it, but she's scared, so finally she grabs it and yells, "Who are you?!"

There's silence on the other end and then a strange voice answers, "I am the Viper, and I am only one block away."

Fig. 6. Photo of Roy, circa 1941. Faintly, he has written of victory on my photo of him: "Hurrah for Victory! V We'll beat 'em." Courtesy of the author.

For a while, there's silence. The woman stares at her phone, but it doesn't ring, and she sighs. *Must have been a prank.* She returns to reading the book that she started a little while ago. The phone rings again. She pauses over the receiver, then grabs it. She holds it to her chest, but even so, she can hear his muffled voice: "I am the Viper, and I am at your door."

The woman runs to her bedroom and locks the door. The phone rings again. She picks it up.

"I am the Viper," the man says in an evil singsong, "and I'm inside your house." No sooner does she put the phone down than it rings. "I am the Viper, and I'm coming up the stairs." She yanks the phone out of the wall and locks the door and she jumps into bed and pulls the covers over her head. She hears the monster outside her bedroom door. "I am the Viper," he bellows, "and I'm standing outside your door!" The doorknob jiggles and she can hear the lock being picked. "I am the Viper," he says, "and I'm in your bedroom." She pulls the covers tighter around her. She hears the monster bending closer.

"I am the Viper," he says softly, "and I'm standing over your bed."

She cowers and trembles as she feels the covers being pulled away, and though she wants to keep her eyes closed, she can't. She opens them and she sees . . . she sees . . . an old man standing there with a toolbox. "I am the Viper," he announces, "and I've come to vipe your vindows, lady."

It's a joke that I have since repeated to my own daughters who, when they were little, would beg me to tell it again and again. I suppose that's because the joke *is* kind of scary, playing on the fears of young children, only to release them from that fear with the dumb punchline. I'm struck too that the Viper makes more sense in today's world than when I was a child, in a time before cell phones. How did this Viper keep calling every step of the way in a world of landlines? No one cared. I certainly didn't. The other men in my family, mostly my great-uncles, told jokes even dumber than the Viper, but I can't remember a single one. Why I can't remember Roy without thinking of this joke baffles me. My mind goes immediately to the Viper when I remember Roy. Not Survivor of Pearl Harbor. Not Murdered in His Sleep by His Own Daughter. He is the Viper Guy.

One summer day, Roy took me and his kids to an amusement park, Rockaway Playland. The family was visiting my grandmother's beach house in Long Beach, New York, as they did every summer. I visited my grandmother, too, every summer, but for the entire summer, not only a few days. He and his wife, Jean, had three kids: Louise, the eldest, who was my age, her sister, Nancy, two years younger, and the boy, Troy. I remember Louise and Troy well, but I have no memory of Nancy at all. I can't picture her face or hear her voice. I can't remember a gesture, an action, only a cool stare. She and Troy sat in the backseat of their station wagon. I rode in the cargo compartment, out of choice, because being unbelted in the cargo area of a station wagon was its own kind of amusement park ride in the days before seatbelts. Louise was with me too as we listened to Roy tell the Viper joke while driving the car, Jean seated beside him. I was glad that Louise sat beside me because I had a crush on her, and I was glad to sit far away from Jean, her mom, who never smiled. Jean yelled at Roy and her kids and seemed not to like any of the people who made up her life. Roy, by contrast, often smiled and laughed and he was entertaining. He seemed harmless, which was about all I ever wanted in an adult.

When we returned from Rockaway Playland, Louise and I sat on the back steps behind my grandmother's house, on a stoop in a little alcove by a dilapidated red toolshed a little bigger than a phone booth. Cats loved to lie on the roof of the shed, and my grandmother would shoo them off, yelling from the porch or the window of her kitchen.

"Do you want to kiss?" Louise asked.

"I guess," I said. I closed my eyes. I didn't know what to do with my hands, so I placed them in my lap.

Louise pressed her lips against mine. I had seen people kiss before, but I hadn't been sure what it accomplished. I opened my eyes. The stoop in the shadows of the shed where we sat was cool and a cat on the roof watched us with mild interest. Then we stopped kissing and went in for dinner. I still wasn't sure what the big deal was. It was no Rockaway Playland.

The next day, the three of us were playing in my grandmother's walled yard, marching around the flower beds and spraying one another with a hose. Louise's brother picked up a cat on its way to the shed and threw it on my back. The cat dug its claws down the entirety of my back and then sprinted into hiding. I screamed and ran up the patio steps to my grandmother's kitchen, trailing the three others, all engaged in blame laying. My grandmother sat there along with Roy and Jean, who asked me what I had done to provoke Troy. My existence was the provocation, though I didn't have words to tell her that. My grandmother brought me to the bathroom to have my wounds cleansed and drenched in the dreaded iodine, which was almost as bad as a cat's claws.

I received a letter from Louise a few years later on April 8, 1974. I remember the date because it was also the day that Hank Aaron hit his famous 715th home run. I was fifteen, working obsessively on my stamp collection while watching our tiny Panasonic TV and reading a letter from Louise, which arrived out of the blue. In the letter, she told me that she wanted to stay in touch because her memories of me were good. My memories of her were good as well and I told myself I would write back to her right away. She told me of her life in New Jersey. She said she had run away, but now she was back. Her mom and dad were divorcing. She remembered how nice I was.

Her letter was warm and engrossed me enough that as I was rereading it, I completely missed Hank Aaron's famous homer. Five years earlier, I had missed the moon landing when I inadvertently took a midday nap, and my kind and treacherous grandmother (treacherous only in this instance) didn't want to disturb me for any old Giant effing leap.

I didn't reply, though I wanted to, and thought maybe I'd call. Yes, I'd find out her number. And call. "I am the Viper and I'm in Indiana."

But I didn't.

The last time I saw Roy was in New York at the apartment of Aunt Gus, then in her nineties. I had shown up unannounced. Feeble and hard of hearing, she tolerated my rude audience with her. There wasn't much to say between our years, and so I kept the visit short. But then a man I didn't recognize joined us. He didn't seem to recognize me either. We shook hands, and then he sat beside Aunt Gus, his hands clasped, arms resting on his legs, head bent—distracted, it seemed.

"Roy," I said as though answering a game show question.

He looked up, still not recognizing me. I had been a runt when I saw him last. "Yes?"

I wanted to say something about Pearl Harbor. I wanted to ask him what was true. Had he really swum underwater? But I refrained.

I saw Roy leaping off the sinking bridge of the *Arizona* into a ring of fire. Holding his breath until his lungs felt like they would burst, he emerged again, took another breath, and dove.

Roy died a couple of years after I saw him in New York. I had recently read of another survivor who died, and whose last request was to join his shipmates in their grave. His request was honored, and he was lowered into the sunken hull. Some events freeze you in time and you can never escape them, and then, instead of trying to escape, you embrace them. You think that you have chosen this fate. You die and lower yourself into the sunken hull.

For years, I didn't know what became of Louise, the cousin who gave me my first kiss, or of Troy, who threw a cat on my back. But the other sister, whose face and features are nothing but a blank to me, whose voice is not even a whisper, had a psychotic break and was committed. And Roy, for whatever reason, took her out of the hospital, claiming that he could take care of her. What happened next was whispered in my family. No one talked openly of it. One night, she went into his room and stabbed him in the heart while he was sleeping.

Beyond those bare facts, I knew nothing else, and I wasn't keen on learning any more. There was no object lesson in Roy's death, except that when someone has survived something miraculous or not survived at all and died in some particularly horrendous way, their lives and deaths often become reduced to that blunt event, at least in the minds of those on the periphery of their lives. That's how Roy was for us, reduced to headlines. "Survivor of Pearl Harbor," as well as "Gruesome Murder Victim at the Hands of His Own Daughter." Every family has its headlines.

When Louise contacted me decades later, she asked if I remembered her. Of course I remembered her. Or I thought I did. I was 90 percent sure she was the daughter I had had a crush on, but I wasn't positive. Perhaps I had just found myself inside a thriller plot in which the murderer, finally out of psychiatric prison, looks up her cousin, an unassuming writer, pretending to be the other sister. Over the months, Louise and I exchanged emails. She had a vivid memory of me as a boy with intense eyes and she recalled the last time we met exchanging knowing looks. I had no memory of these shared glances, but I know what those looks would have been about—both of us were just trying to survive our families. We both had rough childhoods. My father had died when I was seven. My older sister Nola had died of a prescription drug overdose when I was fifteen. Louise and I recognized in one another kindred spirits. We weren't competing to see whose childhood was rougher, but hers still seemed worse. At least my family was a loving one, wrecked as it was.

When we met again in a parking lot in Coralville, Iowa (she was a trucker and passing through with her dog, and asked if I was around. I was), we took a selfie together and I took her to lunch. I asked her about the kiss, but she didn't remember it, which worried me. Had my first kiss been with a future murderer?

There's something about that kiss that I haven't mentioned because it disturbed me for many years. Halfway through our lunch, I found the courage to mention this to Louise to see what she made of it. As soon as we kissed, I told her, Roy appeared at the back door. He seemed to have been spying on us. And I know I'm not imagining this, but she said she would visit me later that evening for more kisses. Louise laughed when I told her this detail. I was relieved I wasn't treading into sensitive territory, though who knows, maybe it was a nervous laugh.

That night, I forgot what she had told me and fell asleep, only to be awakened around midnight with her standing by my bedside. And then Roy appeared again, and he told her to go back to bed. She did so without a word. I remember feeling disappointed, but I wasn't sure why.

Louise had absolutely no memory of any of this.

"Are you sure it wasn't Nancy?" I asked. We had finished eating by then and I had grabbed the check, but I wasn't ready to pay no matter how much our server wanted to clear our booth for the next customer.

"I don't see how," Louise said. "She didn't like people, she was mean, and she never liked to be touched."

"But you don't remember it either."

I didn't want to pry further, but I felt that I needed to ask another question, not so much to satisfy my overactive imagination, but to satisfy the overactive imaginations of anyone I might later recount this story to, with

Louise's permission. I know that sometimes our imaginations are more powerful than the facts. And if I had wondered what Roy's culpability in his murder might be, if he had done something to trigger the attack, I knew that others would wonder as well.

"You know, whenever a young woman kills her father or an older man, there's always the question of something sexual," I said.

She shook her head. "No, that didn't happen. He wouldn't do that. Maybe it *was* me. I responded to anyone who showed me positive attention. It took me a long time before I figured out the best ways to get that." And she laughed again. "I went to visit Nancy once after it happened, and I asked her why. She showed no emotion, and she answered right away, 'I wanted to see what would happen.' I just stood up and walked out."

Louise was sure, too, that Nancy had been the one to tell Troy to throw the cat on my back. Troy wouldn't have done it on his own. *I wanted to see what would happen.*

After the murder, her mother blamed Louise, telling her that it wouldn't have happened if Louise had paid more attention to her sister. But even as a toddler, Nancy showed a mean streak, according to Louise. "One night, when I was five, our parents left me in charge of the other two. Troy was in his bassinet and Nancy kept taking away his bottles. So I would give him another bottle, and Nancy would take it away. By the time our parents returned, she was walking around holding all these bottles. Troy was wailing he was so hungry. My mother blamed me. I was five years old."

Over our lunch, she described a Roy I had never met, known, or heard of. This Roy was neither hero nor victim. This Roy drank every day in a bar next door to his place of work. This Roy passed out in a plate of food at a Howard Johnson's in Paramus, New Jersey, one evening after Louise's mother went to fetch him and thought a meal would somehow sober him up. She was always sending Louise into bars to retrieve her drunken father. On that night, after Jean roused Roy awake, he told her he would only come home if she "[gave] him one of the kids." The kid he was *given* was Louise, who sat petrified in the front seat with him as he weaved in and out of traffic on the long ride home.

This Roy entered the house once, fell flat on his face, and passed out. It was like Dick Van Dyke tripping over the ottoman, except Roy was his own obstacle. Louise just stepped over him and went about her business.

What could I say? I didn't feel that I needed to say anything, but I wanted to say something. Somehow, we had found one another and rekindled our friendship. There wouldn't be any kissing this time. I don't have a lot of relatives left from those days anymore. Almost none. I'll just say that sometimes the broad strokes of a story spare us from coming face to face with something unbearable. Sometimes you need to cover your head with a blanket, but then sometimes you need to throw it off and look around at the world as it is.

There was a lull as we both contemplated what we had left behind or tried to leave behind. I told her that one thing I remembered about her dad was the Viper joke. She didn't remember it at all and she asked me to tell it to her. She said this was her father at his best, his happiest, when he could be gentle and entertaining. So I told her the joke and I took my time with it, embellishing and adding flourishes that I never had before. My Viper accent was pure Vaudevillian. It was the best rendition of that joke I have ever told. I embodied it in a way I never had. I wanted her to know it.

"I am the Viper and I've come to vipe your vindows, lady," I said, loudly enough that a few heads turned in nearby booths.

"Yes," she said, smiling and laughing. "I remember that. I do remember that."

Of the Affection of Fathers for Their Children

To this, such as it is, what I give it I give absolutely and irrevocably,
as men do to their bodily children.
—Montaigne, "Of the Affection of Fathers for Their Children"

Our children haunt us until we die, and then it is our turn to haunt them.
When people are troubled, we say they have "demons," but they're not
demons, only the ordinary sadness and regret that makes life so melancholy
if we survive past the age of forty or so. Anyone who doesn't have regrets is
most likely lying or himself a demon. We don't always feel the same about our
pasts—sometimes a simple memory or an old photograph of our children, the
eldest at five, dressed as Little Red Riding Hood, the other, at three, dressed
as the Big Bad Wolf, facing us from a distance of nearly twenty years, gives
us simple joy. Other times, we contemplate what it means to see them now
after so long, though they can't see us. Unlike in a stranger's photograph, we
have all the context we need, too much context, which floods upon us, and
threatens to tear us from our fragile mooring in the present. Was this taken
before or after the divorce? We wish we could reach inside and bring them
to us just once more as children. Costumed now in adulthood, they can't be
carried around the way they once were. We can't swing them through our
legs. We can barely sit with them in a restaurant without someone thinking
or us *believing* that someone thinks we're cradle robbers, the kind of man
so afraid of his own mortality that he has to be with women young enough
to be his daughter, but not. Some of us *are* that kind of man, or partly that

man—afraid, yes, but please, we're with our daughters, not our girlfriends. And we want to hear everything about their lives, to still be included in some way a part of them, and that's why we lean forward, barely touch our food, find their most banal comment utterly fascinating. Perhaps we're not even really listening to them, but looking for a glimpse of Red Riding Hood or the Big Bad Wolf. Who are these people seated across from us? Please, if you're holding our child, if you've devoured her whole, can you tell us at least if she's okay, if she's being well-treated, if there's anything we can do for her to make this captivity more tolerable?

Some of us have married more than once, and this creates a kind of unthinkable dilemma. Should we have stuck it out with our first wife? But then, the other children we love so much would never have been born. Should we never have married the first time? But then our first children whom we love so much would never have been born. And we never would have missed them, never would have thought of them once, their oblivion only heartbreaking because now it's the last thing in the world we would wish for. And what of those potential children, the children we could have yet with our wife? One more, maybe two. It's not too late, but we don't want to be one of those men whose sons and daughters are young enough to be their grandchildren. We don't want to go to the parent teacher meetings and the talent shows and sit among the other parents young enough to be our children. And we don't want to die before our children really know us. To start haunting them so young seems cruel. Some of us whose parents died young already know this pain. We wouldn't admit this to our wives, but there are times when we can imagine ourselves the man in the restaurant sitting across from the woman young enough to be our daughter, but who isn't. Our wives are not stupid. They know this full well, though there's a tacit agreement that our glances should be brief and circumspect. It's not all about sex, about the biological imperative. Yes, we want more babies. There are more babies to be born, ever more babies, and some of them could still be ours. They're lurking in the wings. We know their potential and they, we suspect, know ours. Maybe we have always wanted a girl. Or a boy. They're remarkable, these invisible children. We care nothing for them now, but give us a good year, and we won't be able to live our lives without them. We will hardly be able to imagine a time before they were born, hardly able to bear the thought of their deaths.

But there are times we have resented them. Times when they were for Raymond Carver "a heavy and baleful presence." That's too strong, too harsh. Never baleful. He didn't feel that way, not really. He loved his two children and never should have committed those words to paper. But male writers who are also fathers, when they're feeling self-pity, that no one loves them enough, are bound to lash out, themselves heavy and baleful presences upon the world. And then they drink or smoke or practice baby-making. Was there anything ever more self-defeating if what we wanted, after all, was affection?

These children wanted nothing but our affection and our affection was always split between them and our other children, the incorporeal ones, the ones who made us cruel, who made William Faulkner tell his daughter Jill, "No one remembers Shakespeare's children." It's a commonplace to say that no one on their deathbed ever wished they'd spent more time at work. But men on their deathbeds have regretted what was still locked away inside them, what they suspected still lurked in the wings. The poet Lucan died reciting his own verses, as Montaigne has it: "a tender and paternal leave of his children, in imitation of the valedictions and embraces, wherewith we part from ours, when we come to die." If his corporeal children were with him at the time, Lucan might well have preferred to embrace them. But these other children he could summon to his side in his need, and they would fly to him. Our embodied children we cannot be so sure of, as King Lear learned too late.

We don't remember Lucan's daughter, alas, if he had one, but we honor Faulkner's poor daughter, who only wanted him to stop drinking, who only wanted a radio by her bed, and Faulkner wouldn't allow her even that, because this would distract him from the children he wanted to survive. We do remember Carver's children, who forgave him for what he wrote in a fit of bitterness. We do remember Montaigne's daughter, Leonora, whom he wrote about so lovingly, and how could he not when all his other four daughters "died at nurse." No wonder he and his wife could never raise a hand against her, could not bear to correct her until she had reached upwards of five years of age, and "then words only, and those very gentle." Another reason to love Montaigne, such a good father—this is what loss will do—who never spanked Leonora because he knew that a child's fear is not a good substitute for a child's love and respect.

Our children don't simply spring from our biological yearnings or our pens, but from our wills, our obligations, and our losses, and to these last we sometimes show the most kindness. When Faulkner's brother died in a plane crash, he adopted his brother's daughter and gave her away at her wedding. In the last five years of Montaigne's life, he adopted a young woman who felt that in his essays she had at last found a kindred spirit. She had lost her own father at a young age, and Montaigne filled this long-vacant role, their relationship as father and daughter one of the most important of his life, that Leonora, though she had every right to resent, apparently didn't. She and Marie le Jars de Gournay became as sisters, though this new daughter was old enough to be Montaigne's mistress and apparently was not. Perhaps her acceptance of this new fully formed sibling stemmed from her own father's kindness toward her and trust in him, a gift repaid.

René Descartes' daughter Francine died at the age of five of scarlet fever, but many years later, when he was summoned by the Queen of Sweden to tutor her, he took passage on a ship and claimed, so the story goes, that he was traveling in the company of his daughter, Francine. The sailors had never seen Francine, and one day they decided to search for her. They found his quarters empty, but on their way out they opened a chest—inside was a girl, or something like a girl. A mechanical doll that moved. The captain, fearing black magic, ordered the doll thrown overboard. And so Francine died a second death and Descartes followed not long after of pneumonia. Whether the story is true can only be the subject of speculation now, but it's been told many times since his death. When it comes to our children, even the "father of modern philosophy," it seems, was as helpless as the rest of us poor fathers.

This is what we want to say to our children. This is what we must say, the fathers of two kinds of children: to the ones whom we should have loved better, or who were taken away too soon by accidents we couldn't have foreseen. *We love you. We love you dearly. We are so thankful you have walked with us upon this earth. But we cannot always be with you. We cannot even always be with ourselves.*

A Reincarnation When I Didn't Want One

A woman with a lopsided smile approached me after class the day my marriage ended. She had dark pageboy hair and ever-scanning eyes, as though reading some invisible teleprompter. "Professor Hemley," she said, almost too quietly for me to hear. "May I speak with you?"

I didn't want to speak with her. I wanted to flee, to take care of what needed taking care of, to start packing, compartmentalizing, rationalizing my way into a new life.

"Of course," I said. "What's on your mind?"

"I read your memoir about your sister, Nola," she said. "It made me remember. I'm pretty sure I'm her reincarnation."

I did not want to be confronted with a reincarnation of my sister, or someone who thought she was, on the day my marriage was breaking up. It was hard enough to process the death of my marriage without having to concern myself with the rebirth of my sister.

"What makes you think that?" I said, gathering my papers and placing them in my satchel.

Her scanning stopped and she looked at me directly. "I just know I am," she said. "By the way," she added, handing me a sheet from Disabled Student Services. "Here's this. I might need some extra time to complete tests and assignments." By law, I couldn't ask anything about her disability, nor could anyone at DSS tell me anything.

I went home to do my packing, but I felt strange when I entered the house. Several decades ago, a bomb was developed, the neutron bomb, that leaves buildings standing but people dead. That afternoon, it was as if the place had been hit with such a bomb; the structure was standing but lifeless.

It's often said that when you face death, your life flashes before you. When your marriage dies, scenes both happy and sad play themselves out at odd moments. On Wimbledon mornings, my wife liked to eat strawberries and cream as she watched the tennis. An Anglophile, she admired British traditions, the reserve and humor of the people, and was addicted to certain BBC comedies (not Benny Hill) and dramas such as *EastEnders*.

Not that that matters to anyone else, but it was knowledge I had of her, something I could expect within our singular marriage that now suddenly made no difference to my life anymore. And I made no difference in her life anymore, she told me.

A couple of weeks earlier, sitting together silently in the living room, a sob had escaped from her—the saddest, most bereft sound I've ever heard. It was the sound of her realizing, as I had much sooner, that our twelve-year marriage was over.

I hurriedly packed, as though fearing my immunity to the bomb would soon wear off. But before I left, I turned on my computer and quickly checked my email. There were several from my student, now calling herself "Janey Butterfly." Given the tone and subject matter, it was a pretty flimsy disguise.

One read: "We have met over many lifetimes, entwined, loving, doomed. Please do not run from me. We must talk soon."

I thought of deleting the message, but then figured I had better keep it.

A few days later at school I received another email, this one from a "friend" of "Janey Butterfly:"

"You have not answered any of Janey Butterfly's emails. You are heartless and cruel, and these actions have not gone unnoticed! The friends of Janey Butterfly, myself included, think you're a meanie. You are going to be sorry."

"I don't mean to be cruel," I wrote to Janey Butterfly's friend, "and I'm sorry if it strikes you that way. But it's inappropriate for you to write to me this way and I would like for you to stop, please."

Shortly, I received a response. "Behind your 'professional' distance lurks a monster. There is something inside you essentially untrustworthy." This last bit she had paraphrased from my memoir.

The next day she didn't appear in class. A relief. I figured she must have dropped it. But the day after she reappeared and stared at me fiercely throughout the hour. I went to my department chairman, who was sympathetic but said we couldn't remove a student unless she was disruptive or caused harm. Well, wasn't she being disruptive and causing harm? Oh, he meant in class. He called up Disabled Student Services and didn't learn a thing. But DSS knew of the situation, from the student's side at least. What was the student's side, I wanted to know? Silence.

The emails continued. Every day, I would receive at least one or two, each castigating me and telling me how sorry I was going to be. One evening, I went to my office in search of financial records I needed for my divorce. It was after 10:00 p.m. and the campus was deserted, the halls appropriately spooky and dark. As I sifted through my papers, the phone rang. No one knew I was there. I let it ring six times, then picked it up.

"It's me," she said. "I want to talk to you. Please stop avoiding me."

"How did you know I was here?" I asked.

She ignored the question, said she loved me and that we belonged together.

I told her that that wouldn't be happening. Trembling, I put the phone back in its cradle.

The next day, I went to my old house and spoke to my wife. I warned her to be careful, that I was being stalked by one of my students and that she might think I still lived there. She listened, concerned, and thanked me for letting her know. I asked her how she was doing. She said she was fine. We had passed into a cordial, if formal, stage.

I called the university's lawyer and spoke to her. She told me she would speak to DSS on my behalf. She also suggested we meet with the campus police—we might need to obtain a restraining order to keep the student away from me. So, I met with the campus police and the lawyer several times over the next few days. I showed them the collected emails and they shook their heads. My department chairman called me in to see him. "Disabled Student Services called," he said. "They wanted me to ask you if you've had a physical relationship with this student. She's suggesting you have."

Never, I told him. But I saw doubt flicker across his face. He knew I was getting a divorce. He was not my friend, but my supervisor. His voice became distant, professional.

After three months of continuing harassment, I finally received a restraining order. My student was not allowed within a football-field length of my third-floor office, which meant that if she wanted to get anywhere near the English Department, she'd have to hover on a cloud outside. The department chairman came to my office one day and asked if I'd show the student mercy and allow her at least to go to the English Department offices. Of course, I said yes.

Meanwhile, my divorce took on a sad life of its own, as divorces tend to do. At one point our court-ordered counselor told my wife and me that we were the most mature divorcing couple she had ever worked with. And it's true we were very well behaved. There were no threats or ugly outbursts, little in the way of arguing. But our divorce was still the most painful thing I had ever been through.

The worst came when my wife announced her intention to take our daughters, ages nine and seven, and move back to her hometown in Wisconsin, half a continent away. I'd expected and hoped to remain in my daughters' daily lives, but the next few short months would be my last, perhaps forever, of living in the same town as them.

In the middle of this awful time, close to the end of the term, I looked up from my office desk to see my student standing silently at my door, staring at me. How long she had been standing there, I couldn't tell. She did not look like the ghost of my sister. She did not look like the ghost of my marriage. She did not look like the faces of my lost daughters. But still, when she said "Boo," I jumped.

The Dachshund Endures

Every day, I picked up Milo, my miniature Dachshund (and minor modernist poet) and brought him to the patio, where I pressed on his bloated bladder and a strong string of pee arced out. Holding him aloft like a communion chalice, I pressed firmly, directing his pee wherever I wanted. On cold days, on rainy days, on hot days, I did this with him several times a day. Sometimes I wrote in his pee on the patio cement. Milo always stayed completely still as I did this, his paws drooping slightly, motionless. It became part of my daily routine.

Shower.

Brush my teeth.

Take out the recycling.

Express Milo.

Odd, he never had any particular expression I could discern as I did this. If you expressed me—of course you'd need to be a giant as I stand five foot eleven and weigh eighty-seven kilos—holding me naked while squeezing my bladder, I would squirm, I would scream. I would be mystified. My penis would retract. Milo's penis was that special alarmed red of dog penises.

Milo endured, his eyes round and wide, but not out of fear, I thought. Sometimes, his right leg trembled, but it did this at other seemingly innocuous times too. Once, while I sat at the kitchen table paying bills, I glanced at Milo dragging his hind legs. He stopped at his water dish and drank, and the muscles of his right leg twitched, as though some race were being run directly beneath the skin. When he was finished, he gave me a look (Do I know you?) and started the journey back to his bed in the living room. Milo stopped midway, trying to turn his head to see what was going on, as poop emerged with locomotive force from his butt. (Does that belong to anybody?)

Milo's malady is not uncommon among Dachshunds, something I wish I'd known when I bought him foolishly and impulsively at a pet store after another dog of mine suddenly died. I didn't know what I was getting into, that Milo would slip a disc when he was five, and that as a result I would have to express him several times a day.

When my first wife and I divorced, she left the state with our children, shedding Milo, a final, parting gift to me. Either that, she said, or he'd have to be put down. I couldn't have that on my conscience, so I took peeing, pooping Milo, plus a closet filled with thousands of catalogs and maybe a hundred cardboard boxes from a shopping channel. It took a wheelbarrow and many trips to get rid of those catalogs.

Many days, I bemoaned my fate, not his. How could I have been reduced to this, squeezing a Dachshund's bladder several times a day? I used to be a grown man with a marriage, a mortgage, children, but it was I who felt somehow reduced to Milo's size. I who felt keenly life's many indignities when it should have been Milo. But it wasn't. Milo endured. I don't know what went on in that miniature brain of his. Not much, I'm sure. To Milo, life was life, pride and indignity irrelevant. We did not understand each other, but we shared these moments nonetheless, both of us single-minded, waiting for something to be finished, and for that pleasant emptiness afterward.

On the Island of Our Fathers' Ghosts

It's an odd sort of person who continues the campaigns of the dead. But there are many of us. War reenactors, battle historians, the children of veterans. The dead often inspire more passion in us than the living. I've come to the island of Corregidor in the Philippines over the years five or six times, taking the same tour around the battle-scarred island on an open-air tourist mover or tranvia, wishing I could stay for more than a day and walk among the ruined bunkers, crawl through abandoned tunnels, and examine at my leisure the giant fallen guns that litter the island. It's an odd wish, I know, but I love history and I love ghosts. For me, history is one long ghost story, and this island has more than its share of both.

I finally get my chance when my friend Peter Parsons tells me that he and a small group are going to spend several days in March to commemorate the anniversary of General MacArthur's return to "The Rock," as American vets who fought there called it. It was from here that MacArthur was spirited away in the early days of the war, when it was certain the island would fall to the Japanese, who invaded the Philippines ten hours after attacking Pearl Harbor.

"I shall return," MacArthur said famously. And: "Old soldiers never die. They just fade away." MacArthur's ghost hasn't faded in the Philippines, where he's still considered a hero. I won't besmirch his name, but I'll just say he had a Filipina mistress nicknamed "Dimples," whom he brought back to Washington with him, keeping her a secret from his mother, and finally paying her off and sending her packing back to the islands.

I'll just say that after he finally obeyed Roosevelt's order to leave Corregidor (the third time was the charm), he left command of his forces on Corregidor to General Wainwright, and expected Wainwright to fight to the end. But Wainwright surrendered in May 1942, sending a wire to Roosevelt stating: "There is a limit to human endurance and that point has long been passed."

I'll just say that after Wainwright was freed from a Japanese prisoner-of-war camp at the end of the war, MacArthur tried unsuccessfully to block Wainwright from receiving the Medal of Honor. What really pissed off MacArthur was that Wainwright ordered other forces not on Corregidor to surrender to the Japanese, countermanding MacArthur's order that they go guerrilla.

I'll just say that during the Korean War, MacArthur wanted to use nuclear weapons, for which Truman sacked him.

I'll just say finally that some of my ambivalence toward MacArthur comes secondhand, from a crusty Filipino tour guide who bent my ear during one tour of Corregidor, telling me how he lobbied successfully for a memorial to Wainwright on the island.

If the wraith of MacArthur wanders anywhere, it's undoubtedly on Corregidor, which seems to have its share of ghosts. Peter and his wife Tea once stayed on Corregidor at the island's only hotel. Out walking one night, a figure dressed in black flashed passed them in absolute silence on a bicycle and then disappeared over a cliff. I've known Peter for many years. He was born in the Philippines, the son of war hero Chick Parsons. When Peter was a young boy, the American soldiers who were captured on Corregidor marched past his family's house. Several soldiers collapsed in the road and he brought water to them. His grandmother, who was helping the guerrilla forces fighting the Japanese, was caught and beheaded. I have no such emotional attachment to the battles that were waged here. My father had a desk job. My ghosts on Corregidor are secondhand.

So on an early sultry morning in March, our driver takes me to Manila Bay where I'm to meet Peter and Tea and the other adventurers who are going to spend the next several days on Corregidor, followed by a jaunt across the bay to the Bataan Peninsula, another famous site of resistance to the Japanese, where thousands of Filipinos and Americans perished in the Bataan Death March. I've begged off this portion of the trip. It's Corregidor that holds me in thrall.

The only practical way to get to Corregidor from Manila is by one of Sun Cruise's ferries—it's about a seventy-five-minute journey to the mouth of Manila Bay, where Corregidor sits. Like nearly all forms of conveyance in the Philippines, you don't go anywhere without an ear-splitting accompaniment. On buses, pirated movies play continuously. In taxis, love songs on the radio. In jeepneys and on motor tricycles, the sound of the engine shakes your teeth out of your head. On the Sun Cruise ferry to Corregidor, a documentary on the war-torn island is cranked up to psychological warfare levels.

Ironically, the island of Corregidor now must be the most peaceful of all inhabited islands in the Philippines. It houses little but the ruins of gun batteries and the shells of barracks; a demolished movie theater; a hospital; the Corregidor Inn; a couple of small snack bars, including the MacArthur Café, all surrounded and sometimes reclaimed by jungle. First used by the Spanish as a fortress, Corregidor was taken over by the Americans who fortified the island shortly after colonizing the Philippines. It's now an island-sized shrine to the Allied dead in the War of the Pacific.

Not many people would want to live on a shrine to the war dead, but Steve Kwiecinski's father was one of Corregidor's defenders. Captured by the Japanese, he survived transport on the infamous Japanese "Hellships," boats that supplied Japan, manned by POW slave labor, and often bombed by American forces. Steve worked as a computer programmer and his wife, Marcia, as a physical therapist assistant until they decided to quit their jobs, sell their belongings, and move to Corregidor. They've lived on the island since October 2008, and they arguably know it at least as well as anyone who has ever set foot there. Steve is tall and lanky like his father and wears a fourteen-size shoe (it's impossible to find a size-14 shoe in the Philippines, he likes to tell people). Marcia's typical hiking outfit on the island consists of running shoes, shorts, T-shirt, and floppy hat. Like Steve, she's fit and equal to the task of bushwhacking jungle trails, searching for lost historic sites, and shimmying through abandoned tunnels. Still, there's something a little odd in encountering a pair of middle-aged Minnesotans living in the shattered ruins (though comfortably in a solar-powered house) of an island fortress.

My other companions include the curator of the MacArthur Memorial in Norfolk, Virginia, James Zobel. Jim has carried with him a forty-eight-star flag (as Alaska and Hawaii hadn't yet become states in the World War II era) from the memorial to be hoisted on the flagpole that MacArthur presided over so many years ago. This is Jim's first visit to the Philippines—the others are veterans, though only one literally so: Karl Welteke. A lifer in the U.S. military, he was born in Germany and spent part of his youth sheltering from Allied bombing raids. Cigar-chomping Paul Whitman from Australia carries a vintage '42 issue Australian machete. His dad was an attorney who was offered a post in the Middle East by a General whom he told, "I wouldn't cross the bloody street with you, you bastard." After that remark, he was offered the choice between a court-martial and a transfer. Luckily, he was a good typist and he wound up on MacArthur's support staff, compiling the daily list of air raids. Finally, there's Lou Jurika, Peter's first cousin, whose father, like Peter's, also fought the Japanese in the Philippines.

The lot of us pile into one of Corregidor Hotel's tranvias and are whisked to Topside, one of the two parade grounds of Corregidor, where a Philippine army honor guard stand in formation, flanked by the U.S. and Philippine flags. Three Philippine officials, one dressed in the traditional barong Tagalog, lay two wreaths, one for Filipino soldiers and one for Americans, on either side of the memorial while the soldiers salute. Steve follows solemnly behind, wearing slacks and a tucked-in Hawaiian shirt. He carries off an impromptu speech admirably, under a drizzly sky, within sight of the gray ruins that dot the island. Even without such a sky and such ruins, even without such speeches, I would find the landscape somber and melancholy in a way that seems most in line with my wistful and restless soul.

I'm not sure why I'm here except that I love Corregidor. I love digging around in history. But I'm not a full-throttle Corregidor buff. I probably wouldn't choose to live here, and my father wasn't a war hero. Perhaps in that way, I'm fortunate. Less to live up to, in this regard at least. I am definitely the least relevant of this ragtag platoon. If this were a war movie, I'd be the new recruit who lands on the island, lights a cigarette, and gets his fool head blown off before he even opens his mouth.

On the first day as Peter and Steve talk about what happened to the men who surrendered on Corregidor, how they were brought first to Manila, and marched through the streets, Peter feels with growing certainty that he, as a young boy, gave Steve's father some water in front of his family's house. Although the soldier was lying down, Peter remembers his great height in relation to the other soldiers. And why not? Who's to say the universe doesn't sometimes deliver such impossible answers to its odd equations? "Thanks, buddy," Peter remembers the young soldier saying, nothing memorable in any other circumstance. "I won't forget that," Peter says, as though the soldier's words were a well-known phrase of MacArthur's.

There's no such thing as an innocent stroll on the island with my companions. Each turn in the road elicits a story of a deadly encounter. Here, at this bend in the road, a group of Americans stumbled upon a group of Japanese. Here, at the top of this cliff overlooking the sea and the beach hundreds of feet below, a group of Americans trying to retake the island in 1945 were pinned against the cliff's edge all night, fending off their attackers. Here at Battery Ramsey is the largest crater on the island, where a two-thousand-pound bomb hit. Here, in the ruins of the movie theater (the projection wall still intact), a makeshift morgue was set up. Here is where the dog tags of a paratrooper who died in the fighting were found only last year.

And here is the bunker discovered by accident ("It wasn't on any map," says Paul), with geckos watchfully on the walls and a swallow's nest and flip flops on the floor and rebar. And here is a cave big enough to stand in, but you've got to dodge the insects and hermit crabs inside, and Paul adds hopefully, "I don't know how many tropical islands you can go to and not expect to be bit by a scorpion or a snake." Ah, but I'm not that easy to scare off. A woman with a basket of cobras once cursed me in India. And scorpions! Ha. I once found a scorpion on the toilet tissue roll in a bathroom on the island of Negros. And I bit its tail off!

Okay, no, I'm getting carried away. I'm fine with anything alive. Just keep me away from ghosts. I don't want any black-robed bicyclists headed my way.

I have my chance to meet the ghosts of Corregidor that evening when we go for an after-dark trek through Malinta Tunnel. This underground fortress was gouged into one of Corregidor's mountains, and from this network, sheltering thousands of men (and a smattering of women, mostly nurses), MacArthur waged war against the Japanese without reinforcements for five grueling and increasingly desperate months. At the end of the war, as the Americans were retaking the island, a large number of the Japanese defenders committed mass suicide by setting off charges in the tunnels. As a result, many of the laterals have collapsed and can't be penetrated, at least not without heavy machinery.

What most tourists see is the main shaft of the tunnel, wide enough to ride several tanks across. It's here that tourists are treated to a "Light and Sound Show." As an announcer tells the history of the siege, tourists proceed along the tunnel in stages, spotlights beaming on successive life-size dioramas depicting MacArthur and Wainwright, MacArthur and President Quezon of the Philippines, nurses tending to wounded soldiers while actors read lines meant to encapsulate what the people trapped here went through. The highlight is when a bombing run is simulated. Lights flicker and go out; the mountain seems to shake as the sounds of bombs explode. It's pretty convincing, but of course can't come close to the real thing. Still, by the end of it, when the spotlights shine on the Philippine flag, I'm always moved.

But tonight I'm in for a tour that isn't scripted or orchestrated in any way. Paul and Karl know these tunnels better than most, and they lead us through a warren of laterals past partially collapsed roofs and piles of rubble into rooms that few people have explored since World War II. I follow at a slight distance from my companions, glancing down empty corridors, walking on my own down an empty part of the hospital, which in 1942 would have been full of wounded and dying men. "The stench in here must have been unbelievable," says Jim Zobel of the MacArthur Memorial. We switch off our flashlights and take in the darkness.

The following day we hike up past cliff-side bunkers overlooking a beach with an abandoned resort, now itself in near ruins, built during the Marcos era on the site of the 92nd Philippine Scouts Garage area, used by the Japanese to concentrate the POWs captured on Corregidor and the other fortified islands in the bay. I suppose it's only proper that this ruin should stand as a memorial on this battered island—why shouldn't greed and insensitivity have its own unmarked shrine? Rumor has it that a group of generals and Korean investors want to turn Corregidor into an upscale condo and golf resort, another money-grubbing travesty. When I hear such things, the idea of becoming a ghost seems almost appealing if one of the perks might be the opportunity to haunt whomever I wanted. I would lobby for some cross-cultural haunting, commuting in the spirit world between Seoul and Manila, doing my best to drive the bastards to their graves too.

But the imbalances and injustices of the material world are probably not so easily corrected, even in the spirit world. The big problem of course is that in time every memorial loses its force and is overgrown by the jungle, by greed, by apathy. Some of my companions feel especially affronted by the Japanese tours that are now offered on the island. When I took my first tour of Corregidor in 1999, Japanese tourists sat uncomfortably in the same tranvias as Filipinos and Americans, but now they're segregated and given a version of history less unpleasant for them. The Japanese tour guide wants to put a Japanese flag on Topside apparently. "I'll tie him to it and shoot him," one of my companions says as we're discussing this. But that's just bravado speaking. The most you can do really is grumble or pee on the foot of the Goddess of Mercy at the Japanese memorial as one of my Filipino guides did once. "They didn't know mercy during the war, when they slaughtered a hundred thousand civilians in Manila," he told me. "Maybe they knew some girl named Mercy. They probably killed her too."

We were standing at the ruins of the hospital when my companion made the remark about tying up the Japanese guide and shooting him. And I'm not trying to be coy when I say I don't remember who said it and I didn't write it down. It could have been any of them. It could have been me. It could have been the ghosts of our fathers. Really, we were all there for them, even me, though my father's biggest war accomplishment was writing *The History of Censorship in the Mid-Pacific* (a classic, I'm telling you!), for which he, Lieutenant Hemley, was given a special commendation from his superiors. I never really knew him because he died when I was only a boy. But I have a desk job too. I'm a writer like him, and I'm out here for him, reenacting and preserving the memory of all those poor guys who died on this island. It's boggling for me to think of all their unborn children, my Never playmates, my Never fellow reenactors. The world is crowded with the ghosts of their collective possibility. As disturbed as this makes me feel, I probably owe my life to the atomic bomb. My father lobbied successfully finally to be shipped overseas and was on his way to be part of the invasion of Japan when the bomb dropped. It's not hard to guess his fate: the Japanese would not have surrendered (of the roughly six thousand Japanese soldiers on Corregidor, fewer than fifty survived) and I would have been nothing but an asterisk in my father's dead eyes on some Japanese beach.

As is my habit, I wander off alone into the ruins of the hospital, looking for relics, looking for ghosts. Like all the buildings on the island, it's a warren of blasted rooms, of stagnant puddles, vines and trees growing from the concrete, staircases to oblivion, and rusted rebar, miraculously, a few rooms intact. I find myself drawn to one in particular, in the middle of the complex, a door leading into pitch darkness. I make my way toward it, my shoulders tensing and shivering, and as I reach in and shine my flashlight, a flock of swallows, perhaps a hundred, shoot past me, some grazing my face and hands. I jump at this apparition, nearly drop my flashlight. Curses are going off in my mind like flares. It takes me a moment on this dark threshold to calm myself, to take stock of what's happened. I've hardly moved an inch since they erupted from the doorway. They're birds, just birds, I know, but all the same, I stop in my tracks, turn around, and head back outside, ready, while there's still life in me, for a promised beer or two at the MacArthur Café.

For the Spirits of Guinaang

When two vehicles meet going the opposite direction along certain stretches of the Halsema Highway in the northern Philippines, one has to back up to a spot where the other can pass. Somehow, our bus driver managed to do just that and allow other buses and trucks to pass a dozen times on our trip without backing off a cliff, though once he was within inches of the edge. There are few guard rails along this mountain trail, and at places the drop-off is a thousand feet. But oh, what a drop into such beauty, down past rice terraces and river gorges and smoky clouds hanging below jagged mountain peaks. I was traveling this treacherous road all because of a story. My traveling companion, Lawrence Reid, had told me this story several years earlier at a dinner party in his condo in Hawai'i Kai on Oahu.

Part of the handle of a gong in his possession was made from the top of the skull of an American GI killed during World War II. The GI was one of two who had escaped a Japanese prison camp and had made their way up north to the village of Guinaang. The people of this village had welcomed the GIs, and eventually the two had moved on to another nearby village, Mainit, which means "hot," so named because of its volcanic hot springs. There, one of the soldiers had taken a wife, and all had been well until one night the soldier named Taylor had become drunk and threw out all the rice stores that one family owned. The village elders decided that Taylor had to be killed, and as it was their practice to take heads, they quickly dispatched Taylor to the afterlife by spearing and beheading him. Seeing that the other

GI was miserable without his companion, they decided to behead him as well so that he could join his friend.

At least one of the soldiers, or part of him, had become a music maker after his death, and I had listened to him make sounds so unlike the sounds he had made in life as Laurie beat him on the gong at the dinner party. Such music often accompanied sacrifices to the spirits in Guinaang, but in Hawai'i Kai its music was more ambiguous, its listeners never having heard such a tune before, made of an instrument of misunderstanding. To have been given such a gift seemed both horrific and something of an honor. But Laurie, of all outsiders, undoubtedly deserved it, and could put such horror in the proper perspective. Reid, a renowned linguist and specialist in Austronesian languages, had been coming to Guinaang since 1959, when as a young lay missionary for the Summer Institute of Linguistics, his job was to learn the local language and translate the New Testament into Bontoc. He lived with the Guinaang people about eight years, earning a doctorate in linguistics in 1966. In 1970, he quit SIL and had taught ever since at the University of Hawai'i, from which he recently retired. Now he lives in Japan with his wife, Ritsuko, also a linguist.

My fascination with the story has to do with the ironies of this particular clash of cultures. By American standards, the people of Mainit had certainly overreacted by beheading the soldiers. But by the standards of the people of Mainit, the Americans had overreacted as well. Laurie related that after the war, American soldiers, hearing of the deaths of the GIs, had come to the village and summarily executed eleven of the village elders.

I'd wanted to make this trip the previous year, but an inconsiderate mosquito had bitten me and I'd come down with Dengue Fever on Valentine's Day as I was having dinner in a restaurant in Manila with my second (and last) wife, Margie. For the next eight days, I languished in a Manila hospital, receiving five bags of platelets, my only company Margie's brother Joe and the BBC on the TV. The theme music of the BBC still makes me feel ill. Margie, of course, came to visit me when she could, but she had to stay at home with our newborn daughter, and so I languished in bed as though I were modeling for the Pietà and received a few doleful visitors, including Laurie.

Over the next year, I corresponded with Laurie, and we arranged to meet in Manila the following May. If it all worked out, he'd take me to Guinaang after all, though we had a short window this time. I was arriving in the Philippines on May 6 and Laurie had to leave for Japan on May 15—if we left on May 9, we'd barely have time to make it to Guinaang, stay a couple of days, and then make the two-day journey back to Manila. National elections were on May 10, not an ideal time to travel, but I had little choice.

On the bus, Laurie told me stories about Pakoran, the man who would be our host in Guinaang. Pakoran had been Laurie's friend almost from the first day Laurie set foot in Guinaang in 1959. In the 1960s and early '70s, the two had roamed widely through the Mountain Province, Laurie negotiating a peace pact between two villages, delivering countless babies and mending wounds, building a couple of airstrips on ridge tops to bring in supplies for the villages. The two had been inseparable.

"Pakoran is a great storyteller," Laurie assured me. "Once you get him going, he won't stop."

When we reached the town of Bontoc, we arranged for a van to bring us the rest of the way to Guinaang. But first, we purchased eggs, vegetables, Spam, and a kind of spirit marketed as a gin but made from cane sugar, called Ginebra San Miguel, all gifts for the family.

The road to Guinaang was good as such roads go. In places, it was cemented, not the entire width of the road, but two strips of concrete set at the width of two tires to run along. The road climbed steadily through pine forests. The mountains, deeply grooved with few ridges but many drop-offs into abysses of varying degrees, shot up at formidable angles from the valley. In the distance, other villages perched on the mountains covered with rice terraces, villages that had been at war with one another off and on for a millennium. Two of the local villages used to gather across the river from one another and hurl stones—if you were hit by a stone and it raised a bruise, that would determine the size of your sweet potato crop that year.

The people of Guinaang had taken the heads of their enemies in the past and stored them in baskets in the back of the group houses where the unmarried men slept. But the last heads had been taken during World War II when the men of Guinaang ambushed a group of Japanese soldiers. The Japanese had come to the village and demanded provisions, but the people of Guinaang told them time would be needed to assemble everything they wanted. While the Japanese soldiers slept in the Anglican Church, the men of Guinaang sent for the resistance forces in Mainit for backup. Throughout the night, whenever a Japanese soldier went outside the church to take a pee, he was quickly dispatched. By the morning, the rest of the Japanese, realizing that no one was returning once they left the church, panicked and fled down the mountain toward the town of Bontoc, first setting the church on fire. But on the way down the mountain, the Japanese were ambushed and every one of them beheaded. The only casualty the people of Guinaang suffered was an old woman lying on her sickbed. The fleeing Japanese shot her out of spite Laurie assumed. Pakoran had been a boy then and had been evacuated with the rest of his family as the Japanese soldiers approached.

"The fellow probably figured he was going to die anyway, so he might as well take someone with him," Laurie said.

In Guinaang, there were bad deaths and good deaths, and losing your head definitely qualified as a bad death. The headless bodies of the Japanese had been buried in the ruins of the church. Normally, such people were buried outside of the village, not under the church, as these men were, which caused a marked decline in attendance at church after it was rebuilt.

I wasn't sure how a group of well-armed Japanese soldiers could be killed, one and all, by spear-wielders. "Apparently, they were terrified of the people in Guinaang," Laurie told me. "They all tried to flee down the mountain, except for one fellow who, instead of running away from the village, ran into it and hid in a house. If the guy had only stayed there, he would have been all right. He would have had to be treated as a guest. But he ran out of the house and tried to hide in a pig shelter. He was easy to kill in the shelter. They simply stood over it and speared him through the thatch."

Scores were still settled in dramatic fashion in the region. Laurie pointed out a road to nowhere across the valley. The road was supposed to connect one village to the outside world, but a neighboring village didn't want the road going through their territory and so had pushed the bulldozers and other equipment over the ledges. A water dispute between Mainit and Guinaang had been resolved when the people of Mainit simply cut the pipe supplying water to Guinaang.

Before the road to Guinaang was built, Laurie used to climb straight up the mountain from Bontoc. The trip took three hours. I didn't see how this was possible.

"Often, we'd make the climb in the pouring rain," he told me. "They used to call me mountain goat back then." Still remarkably fit, Laurie would celebrate his seventieth birthday in several weeks' time. I had never seen a picture of him from his youth, but even now, people remarked on his appearance. He's a trim man with ruddy cheeks and a well-groomed white beard and mustache. When I think of him, I see him smiling. One local man, on seeing us together, wondered jokingly (I hope) who was older, me or Laurie. Although I'm twenty-four years his junior, he's definitely got me beat on posture and weight.

When we finally arrived in Guinaang, I tried to convince myself it was beautiful, but this was a stretch. The village squatted on the mountainside, the small houses sloping down the hillside like seats in a movie theater, the pathways between houses about half as wide as a theater aisle. Certainly, it was in a beautiful setting, but the rusted metal roofs covering virtually every house did nothing to add to the beauty. Forty years earlier, all the houses were thatched, but only one remained now, lived in by an old woman directly above Pakoran's.

Pakoran wasn't home when we arrived, but some of his family greeted us. His wife, Issew, grumbled when she saw Laurie's gift of Ginebra San Miguel. Pakoran, formerly the strongest man in the village and one-time Barrio Captain, was now known as one of the village drunks. When he wasn't drunk, he was still a great storyteller, Laurie said, but by nightfall he was invariably drunk.

Soon, we heard singing coming from outside, and Laurie said, "That's Pakoran."

"He's drunk already," his daughter, Susan, said with false cheer.

Pakoran, dressed in a G-string and a short sleeve shirt with a collar, plunked himself down in our midst, flush with good cheer and Ginebra San Miguel. He smiled broadly at us and spoke effusively to Laurie, often ending a sentence with the words, "Naughty, naughty."

"That's what Pakoran says when he's drunk," Laurie told me. "It's his special word—it doesn't mean anything, but he always says it when he's been drinking."

That night, Pakoran was able to fill in some of the blanks in the story of the beheaded American soldiers, but spoke mostly on the subject of himself and how strong he was when he was younger. "I was the strongest man in the village," he said. "If there was something heavy to carry, they would always say, 'Let's get Pakoran.' I could carry anything. I could carry big rocks. I could carry pigs. Anything you gave me, I could carry."

"They elected me Barrio Captain even though I was uneducated," he told me. "My father was the leader of the resistance in Guinaang during the war, and when they needed someone to run for Barrio Captain, they said 'let's get Pakoran because of his father.'"

Pakoran's monologue went on for the better part of an hour, punctuated by jarring sneezes that ended in high-pitched shouts, another effect, like the word "naughty," of the alcohol. Throughout dinner, he kept up his often incoherent harangue on his prowess, his family and guests tolerant and good-natured about it.

Pakoran stood shakily to search along the wall for his head axe to show me. He soon sat again, empty-handed, which was fine with me. I imagined him severing my knee with the axe. Not that Pakoran had ever used it for its intended purpose. The last man with a chest tattoo, indicating he had taken a head, had died several years ago. This was one of the men who had ambushed the Japanese. To the people of Guinaang, he had been no one special. They were much more interested in the present, in getting food and education, than in the past. The heads of the Japanese and the others kept in baskets at the back of group houses couldn't be looked at in the light or they'd cause blindness. But eventually, the people of Guinaang must have either stopped believing this or thrown out the heads at night, because the heads were long gone, tossed on one trash heap or another or perhaps over a cliff into the river. Or transformed into gong handles. The group houses, low stone structures with metal roofs, are abandoned now.

Sometimes, you could still see old women with arm tattoos, but no one tattooed their arms anymore. The women had stopped when lowlanders made fun of them when they traveled to the city of Baguio.

The next day as we were walking back from a hike to Mainit to take a dip in the hot springs, we ran across a procession headed by a man shouldering a large black native pig trussed up on a stretcher of sorts. At first I thought the pig was dead, it seemed so quiet. The man and the pig were followed by a line of men and boys. We fell in alongside the men and were led to a small courtyard not far from the house where we slept.

The pig started screaming as soon as it saw the knife and continued to scream long after the knife had opened a hole in its throat, its blood flowing into a bowl. It screamed and screamed, though its screams grew weaker and weaker, until it finally died, screaming. You want a pig to make a lot of noise when it's sacrificed. It's the same with killing a chicken. In Guinaang, a chicken is killed by beating it to death. The spirits like the noise.

When the men thought it was dead, they cut off its tail, but the pig was not quite dead and made one last violent and vain attempt to escape. The tail was given to a boy who played with it beside me. The men laid the dead pig across from an old man in a seat who said a prayer over it.

We were asked to contribute money for drinks if we wanted to share in the meat, but I didn't want a share of the meat. Or drinks. I wanted a nap.

I went back to our room and I slept. So did Laurie, and I awoke to a beautiful chorus of men's voices singing a chorale I didn't understand. But I knew it concerned the dead pig. I knew these were prayers offered to the spirits to accept the gift of this pig.

It sounded like a great chant to me, but it turned out to be pretty average as these things go. Laurie said they were doing the first prayer correctly, but that wasn't hard since it was completely ad lib except for the tune. When they started the second prayer, they couldn't get it going. Even Susan noticed this and said to Laurie in Bontoc, "They've forgotten the words." Well, that was a disappointment. I'd seen a pig sacrifice, but it hadn't been a particularly good pig sacrifice. In a couple of generations, after they stabbed the pig in the throat, they might be singing, "We will, we will rock you!"

Ever since attending this pig sacrifice, I've noticed ads in which a cartoon animal happily invites humans to eat members of its own species who are not cartoons: a cartoon chicken smiling over a headless frozen chicken carcass, a pig licking its chops over a line of tasty sausages. Before this, I hadn't noticed. Like hungry, headless ghosts. Out of spite perhaps, death, even of their own kind, pleases them.

The next day we took a jeepney to a village with spectacular rice terraces. The jeepney was packed with people and their goods and we could only travel on top of the roof—soon I had nestled (though "nestle" is perhaps too comfortable a word) on top and between some sacks of rice and in this way, I jounced and clung on while we traversed another treacherous mountain path. After half an hour or so, Laurie yelled that we were coming into town. I nodded. And then he told me to duck and I looked ahead and saw a wire of some sort strung across the road at exactly the level of my neck. I lay flat across the bags of rice a few seconds before the wire and I met—had Laurie not warned me, the wire would undoubtedly have beheaded me.

I'd like to say that I wasn't ready to be beheaded that afternoon. But who is? You don't expect to be beheaded when you leave the church to take a piss. You don't expect to be beheaded when you get drunk and misbehave a little. You don't expect to be beheaded when you're going on a tour of the rice terraces. Such stories are much more enjoyable when they're someone else's story, not yours. Understandably, the incident spooked me a bit, and I didn't quite feel right for the rest of the afternoon.

After we'd hiked the terraces, we came upon an ancient woman, probably one of the last to have tattooed arms. Wanting to snap her photo, I asked Laurie to politely make the request. Nearly deaf and completely blind, she managed nonetheless to understand, we thought, then wrapped a cigar, lit it and began to rant quietly. She seemed in conversation with the air, with memory as she waved her patterned arms through the billows of smoke she created. She hardly seemed to know we were there and we hardly seemed to know she was there or thought her already gone and the people around me, including Laurie, said, go on, take her picture, and I guess I needed proof that we both still existed. So I did. Everyone else at the stop laughed at her, crazy old woman with the tattooed arms. They told her she must go home, that she couldn't stay anymore in the small store where she was resting. She stood uncertainly and began her walk back home along the walls of the rice terraces, back to her distant village. If she fell the twenty or thirty feet from one of the terrace walls, she'd likely die, and perhaps it's precious and sentimental to think that she knew the path so well that she'd never lose her way. People fall and injure themselves and die sometimes in Guinaang, I can report with virtual certainty, though most often out of sight of the fortunate visitor. The fact that you know a path well does not necessarily make it less treacherous.

That night at dinner, I didn't learn anything more from Pakoran about the two beheaded soldiers. He had been drunk since breakfast but told us that friends his own age were already dead and that he wasn't going to die. He was far too drunk to relate anything in coherent fashion. Pakoran curled up and nodded off to sleep in front of us and everyone seemed relieved, not least of all his wife, Issew, who smiled wearily after spending the entire day bent over in one of the rice fields, where by tradition only the women work.

I heard something fall behind me and I thought maybe someone had dropped a cooking utensil. "What's that?" I asked.

"Oh, just a rat," said Susan with such a big smile that I thought she was kidding.

The rat jumped out onto my foot as though incensed by my doubt of its existence. Then it jumped on Laurie's foot and we all yelled and the rat scurried off to another corner of the room. Only Pakoran didn't stir.

At breakfast the next morning, a toddler named Dexter was occupied with a giant beetle he'd found. He pulled off a couple of legs, then let it crawl on its remaining legs over his hands. Dexter held the beetle out before him, wanting the adults, including me, to share in his delight, every once in a while letting out a roar that seemed to herald his self-appointment as king of the beetles. I tried to strike a balance between good-natured approval of his find and adult reticence, not wanting to encourage too close an alliance between me and Dexter and his lone, tortured subject.

Pakoran wasn't there to say goodbye. He was in the next house, screaming his head off. I could hear Issew talking in calming tones to soothe him, but it did no good. Delirium tremens had hold of him—what poisoned version of himself he was trying to scream out of his being I couldn't know, but it alarmed even Dexter, who sat by the side of the house, saying nothing, the beetle now motionless in the dirt.

"I've never seen Pakoran like this," Laurie told me. "I've never seen him this bad."

Before we left for Manila again, Pakoran's daughter Susan handed Laurie a short essay she'd written in her native language. Laurie had asked Susan to write the essay, not because he wanted to encourage her as a budding memoirist, but because he wanted to see how much Ilocano (the language of the lowlanders) had infiltrated the local Bontoc language. Many words, it turned out. But what interested me were not the changes in the language, but what Susan was trying to tell us. The story Susan had written, I learned later, concerned the problems facing the youngest child in a family. When the girl in the story was younger, she had known her father had loved her and she had loved him. Now he was drunk every night and she didn't know his feelings for her anymore. She had gone away to school in Sagada, happy to be away from the family, but then after a year, she had missed them and cried every night, and now she had returned. The old feelings were starting to come back. Sometimes she wished her father would just go ahead and die.

A few months later, that's exactly what Pakoran did—and while I didn't know this would happen so shortly, it seemed the general direction in which he was headed.

A man who was stumbling drunk yelled some good-natured nonsense as Laurie and I boarded a Bontoc-bound jeep by the church. The man was probably thirty years Pakoran's junior, but he was starting young. Another man was led carefully to the front seat where he sat with his mother. His expression was completely blank. He had a deep wound on top of his head and looked as though he was dead already. He stared straight ahead. Nothing moved him. He made no sound and acknowledged no sound, though first his mother tried to talk to him and then his father, standing by the window. He seemed to be looking off into the afterlife, not at the road in front of him, not at his loved ones or life in Guinaang. Would he be able to hear the pleas of the living as a spirit if he was beyond listening while yet alive? The night Taylor and his friend died, the people played gongs all night long. Much later, in Hawai'i Kai, I heard the faintest echo of death's music.

The jeep started up and we rumbled and jostled with a full load of passengers. Slowly, we began our descent into the valley. I couldn't wait to leave this village, which seemed somehow infested with mortality. I didn't fancy myself a connoisseur of death. I wanted to go back home to my land, where people recover, where they pretend they'll never die.

Feast for the Departed

Auntie Eppie has returned from California, which she found too cold. Auntie Joven, who carved herself a new lifeline, has returned from the mountains of Bukidnon where she has been searching yet again for Yamashita's treasure. Uncle Johnny's widow, Linda, has returned full of contrition from familial banishment because she received a sign from the husband she probably killed through neglect (three drops of blood that rained from nowhere and fell in front of her face). Uncle Boy's wife sits at the table of my mother-in-law, hours before the festivities begin, because she wants a free lunch. Only Evil Auntie Neneng won't attend because she has not been invited, because she is Baby Burgos's mortal enemy. Baby's close friend Mrs. Hamdan, a Muslim, prepares the dishes for the party, including various pork dishes. "She can cook it," Baby, my mother-in-law, tells Margie, my second (and last) wife. "She just can't eat it."

I say nothing. I saw the pigs taken away yesterday, and have lost my appetite for meat in general, pig in particular. "As of this moment, I'm a vegetarian," I told Margie. I'm a Jew, but I would still eat pork prepared by a Muslim cook. Normally.

The two pigs were calm until the men came for them by the fence and then the pigs started screaming as though they knew they would not see the sun set. We all went to the porch as two men threw them to the ground and trussed them to the back of a motorcycle-trike. The first pig stopped its screaming once it was trussed and lay in the trike, hopeless. The goats went without much of a fuss at all. My sister-in-law Malou burst into tears, but she'll cry over anything, and the rest of the family laughed at her. Even I was a little surprised. She grew up here in Mindanao. This is not a place for squeamish people.

The first time I visited Margie's family in Kidapawan was in an army truck, though not because we needed it. We were just hitching a ride. Traveling by bus in advance of a nationwide transportation strike, the strike caught up with us one stop away from Margie's hometown, in Makilala, a hotbed of communist insurgency. No matter. An army truck was there to meet us when the bus stopped, and we piled in. Margie advised me to keep my head down (I did) and blend in (I didn't).

The pigs' heads hang on nails, their expressions docile again, presiding over the cooking of their bodies. Eventually, the heads will find their way into one dish or another. Uncle Boy's wife, Linda, sits at the table with her family eating pork, though the party won't begin for another six hours. Uncle Boy won't show his face because he's a drunk, and even the day my father-in-law died he was shouting insults from the adjacent yard. But my mother-in-law is generous and forgiving and won't turn away his family. Still, I turn to Malou. "I thought Filipinos are supposed to be late," I say.

"That's true," she says. "They came early because they didn't want to cook. They wanted to eat our food."

After lunch, we pile into the van to visit the grave of Baby's late husband, my father-in-law, Joemarie Burgos. Throughout the 1970s, '80s, and much of the '90s, he eluded bombs and guns as a national police officer in the wild, wild South of Mindanao where he battled communist and Muslim insurgents. Margie likes to tell of the time her father was supposed to go on patrol, but was asked to stay behind by his commanding officer to take the v150 armored vehicle he was in charge of in for maintenance. In doing so, he escaped an ambush. Every member of his team was killed, their bodies dismembered. What caught up with him was his own *matigas ang ulo* (strong-headed) nature. He suffered a stroke, wouldn't give up smoking, suffered another stroke, finishing what the rebels couldn't.

You might imagine that such a man would have children of a similar nature, and you'd be right. Was there any question that I'd be attending his third death anniversary in bomb-laden Mindanao? There was none.

Mention to most Filipinos (especially those in Manila) that you're traveling to Mindanao, and they act as though you'll never be heard from again. Perhaps my attitude toward terrorism and mayhem is a bit too laissez-faire—but I view all of this, and by "this," I mean life in general, as a matter of timing. A year after we visited a high-end resort called Dos Palmas off the coast of the island of Palawan, the terrorist group Abu Sayyaf raided it and took several Americans hostage, one of whom they beheaded almost immediately, and the other, missionary Martin Burnham, who died, caught in the crossfire, as he was being rescued.

My mother-in-law's house was built on the Japanese garrison from World War II. Her father was nearly executed by the Japanese but was saved when allied planes flew overhead and the Japanese guards fled in terror. That's the way it is with this place. It's no place for the squeamish.

At the family plot, a gated enclosure with a metal fence and about ten well-tended graves made of tile and stone, Baby steps out of the van and says "Hello" in the general direction of her departed family. She takes my youngest daughter, one-year-old Naomi, from her seat and carries her to the gravesite, followed by the rest of the immediate family, as well as the driver and a helper who carries a large bucket of water, much of which has sloshed out during the five-minute trip, and soap. The driver and helper wash the grave of my father-in-law, a blue tiled slab near the front of the small cemetery. The other graves tell the fortunes and misfortunes of Baby's family—front and center are her illustrious parents. Her mother was "queen" of the Manobo tribe and most of the land around the graves used to belong to the family, but now it has been lost to squatters and Evil Auntie Neneng. Baby's brother, Datu (chief) Joseph Sibug, likewise rests here—a Marcos-era congressman, he married Neneng, who since his death nearly two decades ago, has steadily sold off the family lands, forging documents and signatures to do so. She regularly puts curses on Baby's family—Baby's sister, Auntie Joven, the treasure hunter who once carved herself a new lifeline, was one of those cursed, and would have died if not for the intervention of a "quack doctor." I've never met Evil Auntie Neneng, but in the cosmos of the Burgos family, Neneng looms as large as Voldemort: "I'll see you in hell," she told Baby last time they met.

On the way home, we take the "Gone with the Wind Tour," surveying the lands that used to be Baby's, but which Neneng sold.

"Did they have the title?" I ask.

"I don't know. When Daddy died they took all the papers with them."

"And all Mommy and her sisters do is to go 'ninininininini' instead of doing anything," says my sister-in-law, Tricia, her hands imitating yakking mouths.

"That's because we were putting all the kids through school. We didn't have the funds to fight." She points to the shacks of her remaining tenant farmers and one lone banana tree standing in a field. "My tenants are very lazy. That's my banana plantation."

We need a few more things from the market and so we head to the center of Kidapawan City. Like most provincial Philippine towns of any size, Kidapawan is congested, smoky, and noisy, especially around the market area where scores of motorized pedicabs ply the main thoroughfare with their mosquito engines. Last time I was here, a bomb went off right after our visit in front of the travel agent where we bought our return tickets. Another time, we toured a bomb crater left near the bus station. Another time, a bomb went off at the "waiting shed" of the Davao airport not long after we left that same airport.

"Have there been any incidents lately?" I ask, trying to code my language so that my six-year-old daughter, Shoshie, won't be alarmed.

Margie shakes her head. "No new incidents," she says, pointing out the new pedestrian bridge near the market.

Baby turns around from the front seat. "Oh, there was a bombing right here last week," and points to the bridge we're passing.

"Ancient history," I say to Margie.

At the house, we gather to pay our respects to Joemarie, the living room packed with relatives and friends of Baby and many others who just want food. The remains of pigs and goats in many forms line the table along with rice and cakes and vegetables. Among the guests are some of my brother-in-law Joe's old classmates from grade school, his barkada. They're mostly policemen, one on duty shouldering an Armalite because the area is on high alert.

Baby took in Auntie Joven's children when Joven's husband, a Muslim policeman, turned renegade and was shot and killed by his former colleagues. Joven went off to the mountains in search of lost gold but now has returned to fight Auntie Neneng for their lost lands. She doesn't look like much of a fighter, as now in her sixties she wears a fluffy dress and has dyed blonde hair, but none of them do really.

With karaoke microphone in hand, she makes a long speech about the love between her sister and Joemarie. "Love conquers all," she concludes, and while I don't necessarily buy that because I'm not the sentimental type, my adopted family has convinced me at least that love is a ceasefire, a lull in hostilities. Still, a Kevlar vest isn't a bad investment.

After the many speeches, we eat because as my mother-in-law says, "In the Philippines, we always remember our dead with food."

And so we do. We remember Joemarie until our stomachs are so full we can eat no more. In other ways, too, we remember. My sister-in-law Malou remembers by scolding a group of teenage boys who left their plates of food on the table and had their feet up disrespectfully on the furniture. Margie remembers by denouncing Uncle Boy's wife who is back in the kitchen packing up more food to bring home to her husband and as we will later learn, to Evil Auntie Neneng. "Hey," she yells toward the kitchen, "Those people who pack up food once shouldn't pack it up again!" Even Margie's sisters are a little scandalized by my wife's boldness. I tear off a little pig skin and head outside to join the drunken police.

In the Storeroom of Petty Hatreds

I was raised to be charming, not sincere.
—Prince Charming, *Into the Woods*

I have a mean bone in my body. Multiple mean bones, in fact. For instance, I hate people who smile all the time. It feels good to say that word "hate," doesn't it? Would you like to try it? Say: "I hate people who ask rhetorical questions that can't possibly be answered." Or form your own. Start a sentence with "I hate people who . . ." or even take out the qualifier and just say, "I hate people. I wish them all ill." It releases something, though there is always more hate to take its place. Actually, I smile all the time, and that's one of the things I hate about myself, though this is not an essay about self-loathing. Not really. It's just that I'm not above hating myself, and I want you to know that.

Because I know you care.

Constant smiling is a loathsome American habit. Underneath lives a bitter and unhappy person. You can bank on it. Millions of bitter and unhappy people walk around the U.S. smiling all the time. This is why Europeans hate us so, or pity us at the very least. How can we be trusted?

You can trust people in photos from a century and a half ago, but not people in contemporary snapshots. A century and a half ago, it was not the habit of people to smile when their photos were taken. Smiling for the camera is a recent convention. *What are you smiling at, you idiot?* a mother of a century and a half ago might scold her child smiling at the camera. "Life is hard." I don't hate these people of a century and a half ago. They're all dead anyway.

I do not remember the first person I hated, but I clearly remember the first person who hated me. David Roger Biddle. I was ten and he was seven when David Roger Biddle moved into my neighborhood. On the first day he saw me playing in my front yard, he strode over to me, stood ten paces away, and waved. He was dressed in shorts that puffed about his waist and a red shirt with a wide collar, black shoes and white socks. His light brown hair was slicked down and perfectly parted. "Ha, ma name is David Roger Biddle," he said.

"That's interesting," I said and ignored him.

The next day, he came over again. "Ha, ma name is David Roger Biddle."

"What is it?" I asked.

"David Roger Biddle."

I told David Roger Biddle to wait for me and I went inside to get my brother.

"Ha, ma name is David Roger Biddle," he told my brother.

For the next two weeks, I tried to see how many times I could get him to say David Roger Biddle. I never tired of hearing him say it. He never tired of saying it and never varied the way he said it. I'm sure there's not another single kid from my childhood whose entire name I committed to memory.

One day, my family and I returned home from an outing to find our front door open and a line of my toys stretching from our yard to the yard of David Roger Biddle. The line of discarded toys ended at the mouth of the well in the Biddle's front yard. Into these depths, David Roger Biddle had cast most of my toys.

The checkout clerk at Walmart tells me to smile on the rare day I'm not smiling. "Smile," she tells me, as though she really cares. "It can't be that bad." How does she know? But I do as I'm told. I smile and I go away hating us both and vow never to set foot in Walmart again, whose mascot, in any case, is a smiling yellow dot. What makes yellow dots so happy anyway?

Tell me your good news. I'll pretend to be thrilled, delighted, overjoyed. A new car? Your dream house? You sold your novel to the movies? I'm so *happy* for you! I tell you my good news and I know you secretly hate me, wish me nothing but ill. I know it's a sin, but it's not easy to remember. That's why God had to write it down for us.

I'm Justin and I'll be your server tonight! Can I start you folks off with a drink? How about one of our signature Margaritas? And may I recommend the Nachos Especiale?

I often laugh nervously. If you say something hateful to me, I will undoubtedly laugh nervously, then go away and feel hurt, which will then become hate, both inner and outer hate, and some of it will be released later as gossip about you and some of it will stay inside, chugging away. Little murdering engine of meanness.

Yes, I know hatred is self-destructive. That's nothing new. But this knowledge makes my hatred no less relevant, no less plausible, no less necessary. You expect this essay to turn around, don't you? You expect me to admit that hating others *only* hurts myself. But no, this essay will not give you the satisfaction. Find it somewhere else.

Last year, one of my oldest and dearest friends, Stuart, told me that he'd discovered that his wife, also one of my oldest and dearest friends, had been having an affair with a colleague for the past two years. This man was not only a colleague of Stuart's wife, Beth, but a friend of Stuart's as well. They'd shared meals, even vacations, had traveled the previous summer to Europe together. All this time, even in Europe they'd been carrying on, and he never knew until one day he picked up the phone extension and listened. Remarkably, Stuart and Beth had stayed together, she contrite, he terribly hurt but as forgiving as he could be.

"Do you hate him?" I asked Stuart recently.

"Well, I don't ever want to see him again," Stuart admitted, "but do I hate him? What's hate?"

He proceeded then with a meandering philosophical discussion. He mentioned that this man called him the week before Yom Kippur, the Day of Atonement, when Jews are supposed to ask forgiveness for their sins not only from God but from those they've personally injured, and asked him for forgiveness. "What happens if I forgive you?" he asked the man. "Do you feel good about yourself then?"

I told Stuart I wouldn't have the nerve to do what this other man did, not that I admired him. I might be petty, but I'm loyal to my friends. But it's easy to admit your faults to God. To admit your faults to those you've actually injured? Can you imagine the fallout, the general befuddlement and panic an outbreak of begging forgiveness would cause if such a practice became widespread? How hard it would be to hold on to your hatred—but surely not impossible.

Did he hate his wife? I asked. No, because there's a shared history between them, and many good things in the past, and many good things hopefully in the future. A certain part of him knew it was biological. Maybe he would have done the same in her situation.

"Do I hate him?" he asked again. "I don't think so. But do I wish him evil? Yes, by all means. I wouldn't mind if someone broke both his kneecaps."

While watching the local news, I wait for the moment before the commercial when the camera, lingering a second too long, captures the weatherman's true countenance. His smile drops, his eyes harden and two zones of high and low pressure converge.

I gave a community writing workshop years ago in Charlotte, North Carolina. It was in a church basement, and I was wearing my Community Giver face that day, the happy face of the motivational speaker who gives workshops to retired people and tells them that everyone has a story inside them, something valuable to share. Am I an impostor? Sometimes. Are you an impostor? Probably, sometimes.

A recently retired banker was among the twenty or so participants that day, and after the workshop he approached me and said he wanted to ask me a question. I thought it would be about how to get his novel published, but no, he told me that when he was twenty or so in the late 1950s, he'd taken a trip around the world and had spent a month or so bumming around India.

There, he'd run into two other Americans, a couple of men a little older than he. The two men were lovers and at first they were friendly to him and they traveled around India together for the next couple of weeks. But as time went on, the two started making fun of him mercilessly, acting so cruel that he came to hate them.

"One of them was a writer," he told me, "and I was wondering if anything became of him." This was a time before a search engine could easily have answered his question. I could see in his eyes what he was hoping, that he'd mention the name and I'd say, "Nope, never heard of him."

"His name was Allen Ginsberg," the man said.

"Are you kidding?" I asked.

"You've heard of him?" he asked.

"He's one of the most famous poets of the twentieth century," I told the man.

"Oh, well," he said. "I was just wondering."

I felt bad for him, but what could he do? Take all of Ginsberg's poems and throw them in a well?

The clerk approaches like an Irish Setter. If he had a tail, he would wag it. Upon turning one's gaze on him, he might squat and pee.

"If you need anything, just holler," he says. "My name's Jeff."

Ten minutes later, I have a question for Jeff so I saunter over to the counter. He has his back turned to me and he's chatting with some of his coworkers. His voice is not the friendly voice of the Jeff I know and love, but low and mocking.

"Hey Jeff!" I holler like he told me. "I need some help."

Jeff turns around, clearly shocked. His eyes go hard and his voice becomes formal. What? He didn't mean it? None of those honeyed Jeff-sonian words? He was stringing me along all this time?

Oh Jeff, Jeff, JEFF! How I hate you!

"I'll be with you in a minute, sir."

At that same community workshop, I met a man who claimed to be a film producer. He and his wife had recently moved to the area because his wife was in charge of a big studio theme park that had recently opened in the area. He told me he had read my novel and was interested in making it into a film. "But of course the ending would have to be changed," he told me. "It needs to be more uplifting."

"Of course," I agreed.

He had loaned out his copy of the book, he said, and he wondered if I might have another. So I gave him the one I had with me. But I had a feeling he would take my book and that would be the last I ever heard from him.

He took my book and that was the last I ever heard from him.

Perhaps he died in a terrible accident on the way home from the workshop and that's why. One can only hope.

In that same novel, I put the names of people I disliked on gravestones. I thought of it as some clever revenge, but it worked differently. I buried my animus toward them. Or maybe time did that.

It's been our pleasure serving you today. We've truly enjoyed having you on our flight and we hope to see you again in the near future and that you have a wonderful day in Salt Lake City or wherever your final destination might be.

The novel had its genesis as a short story—an ambitious story told from several points of view. A failed story. I wrote the story while a Fellow at a prestigious arts colony for young writers, and the day I finished it, I ran into a visiting former Fellow, who complained that none of the current Fellows were showing her any of their work.

"I just finished a story," I told her. In fact, I had "finished" it a mere thirty minutes earlier.

"I'd love to see it," she said. She smiled sweetly and so I handed her the story.

That night, I had a nightmare. I dreamed that not only did she hate the story, but she thought the story was terrible, wretched, pathetic. In my dream, she berated me mercilessly until I was nearly in tears. But as they say in terrible, wretched, pathetic stories, it was only a dream, and I awoke.

But it wasn't only a dream. When I met her, she was worse than the dream. She told me that I had no talent, that it was the worst story she'd ever read, that she was shocked I'd been allowed into the place.

So, of course, I turned the story into a novel and I tried to forget her.

Years later, I wrote a memoir about my sister. By coincidence, she wrote a memoir about her sister that was more successful than mine. Then I wrote another nonfiction book and, by coincidence, she wrote a nonfiction book with almost the exact same title as mine. Hers was on the *New York Times* Bestseller list for a week. Mine wasn't.

Did I hate her? What's hate? Did I wish her evil? By all means. If someone had broken her kneecaps, I wouldn't have minded.

I'm her David Roger Biddle:

Hatred is a place you touch from time to time. Mostly, you forget it's there, but then something reminds you and you touch it again, you worry it with your tongue, poke it with your finger. Why? Why can't you just leave it alone? Maybe it won't heal, maybe it will always be there, but do you have to keep touching it all the time? For heaven's sake, people are watching.

In the life of my rival, the woman who does not even know she is my rival, there is some hatred she is nurturing. Of this, I can be sure. But it's not me she hates. She barely knows I exist. Because we are human, we need hatred. We don't want it necessarily. We don't like it, but it's there, and the more we try to deny it, the more it returns. It's gossip, betrayal, pride. It's the certainty that someone has it better, that life is unfair and that we've paid our dues, which makes us even bigger fools. Dues for what? So we can be happy yellow bouncing dots?

"Smile! C'mon, smile! It won't kill ya!

There ya go! Now, was that so terrible?"

PART 3

Salvage Projects

How to Remove a Curse

The old woman, dressed in a sari and covered in silver bangles, placed a basket beneath my eyes and opened the lid. Inside, dozens of baby cobras writhed. I stood in a crowded market in the town of Shimla, in the foothills of the Himalayas, waiting for Margie and Shoshie while they shopped in one of the small stores that packed the narrow lane. Pulling stroller duty with Naomi, I had been trying to stay out of the way of the steady flow of people crossing my path in both directions. The woman said something to me in a language I didn't understand, and held out one hand while keeping the basket of snakes close to her chest with the other. A basket of cobras is more effective a panhandling technique than most, and so I reached into my pocket to give her some rupees.

I used to catch snakes as a kid in Ohio and snakes don't bother me. Spiders either. I have a healthy fear of heights, but nothing I'd classify as a phobia. I've even had a rifle held on me in Mindanao and I think I handled myself with an aplomb that surprised me. Not that I'm brave. You wouldn't look at me, not quite six feet tall, with a bit of a gut, and say, "Now *that's* a macho dude." I'm just saying that the things that should scare me usually don't and the things that shouldn't scare me sometimes do. By "things that shouldn't scare me," I mean largely the supernatural.

At that moment, Margie emerged from the shop along the way and she signaled me to join her. I asked her to wait but she seemed impatient and was already moving along in the crowd. She has a habit of disappearing, and while that's okay in a grocery store, I didn't want to lose her in a crowd in India. I put my wallet back in my pocket and the woman with the basket of snakes let out a horrified shriek as if I had bitten her, followed by a cascade of words for which I needed no translator. As I picked my way through the narrow street, she followed, keeping up a steady flow of shouts. People around us stopped and gaped. Part of me wanted to simply give her some money, but ahead of me, Margie was already being swallowed up by the swell of people and I didn't want to lose her.

When I finally caught up with her, she asked me what *that* was about back there and I told her that I thought I had just been cursed. She laughed and waved the curse away, though of the two of us, she believes more readily in curses than I do. Just not on that day.

The only place in the Philippines more likely to leave you accursed, besides Margie's birth island of Mindanao, is the fabled island of Siquijor, the Isla del Fuego of the Spanish, where black magic and white magic practitioners reportedly abound. Curses run rampant in Margie's family line. The chief purveyor of curses is Evil Auntie Neneng. By some accounts, Evil Auntie Neneng's husband died not of complications from diabetes, but more certainly because he was cursed by Evil Auntie Neneng, who immediately took up with another man and started grabbing the family lands that rightfully belonged to Margie's mother and her siblings. Over the years, she has employed thugs to murder those who would stand in her way and has sought more arcane methods to fulfill her agenda as well.

Margie's Auntie Jovan, for instance, fell deathly ill one day for no apparent reason. Her head pounded and she could barely stand. After three days of this, a friend of hers sought the help of an itinerant Indonesian healer who, upon gazing into his crystal ball, saw a coffin. He determined that Jovan had been cursed and that it was a good thing that he did not see a wreath of flowers laid upon that coffin or his help would have come too late. He instructed the friend to bring him such a wreath to counteract the spell. When he described the person who had cursed Jovan, the description perfectly fit Neneng. Of course.

If I seem skeptical, well, that's the nature of curses, isn't it? Margie is skeptical of my curses and I'm skeptical of hers. That's the default when it comes to curses. It's a matter of belief, goes the conventional wisdom, and if you don't believe, you won't be affected. And it's easy to disbelieve if you're not the one who's been cursed.

Curses most often belong to the dispossessed, their last and ultimate defense. The best curses come from those who have a history of oppression. Think of the Roma in Europe, Haitians, Afro-Cubans.

"Can curses pierce the clouds and enter heaven?" Queen Margaret asks in *Richard III*.

A curse is a last resort, when earthly justice fails, an act of desperate rage that requires no surefire answer from God as to its efficacy. The curser curses first and takes credit later. In Margaret's case, her question is rhetorical. She expects no answer except in results. Both her husband and her son have been murdered. What does she have to lose? "Why, then, give way, dull clouds, to my quick curses!" she cries. In her case, God listens and all those who have had a hand in the deaths of her husband and son eventually meet their ends just as she has predicted.

Rarely are the effects of a curse quite so transparent or tidy. Some of the best curses arguably come from my ancestors, those who cursed in Yiddish. Oddly, on the day of my brother's wedding, my great-uncles, Morty and Bill, sat with me on my grandmother's porch in Long Beach, New York, and taught me all the Yiddish curses they knew. To this day, I'm not sure why they chose a happy occasion on which to spout curses, except that this side of my family was a dour lot, and too much happiness perhaps put them ill at ease and they needed to counter with some good old-fashioned spite.

Lie with your head in crap and grow like an onion.

May you give birth to a trolley car.

May you have two beds and a fever in each.

If the curses of the Jews are colorful, they're also easily ignored. How can you take such clever curses seriously? They're infected by a built-in self-consciousness. "May you give birth to a trolley car"?

The forebears of my people, the Israelites, cursed better or at least more earnestly. Here, the prophet Elisha curses a bunch of rambunctious boys:

And on his way up to Beth-El, he encountered some small boys from the city who mocked him, "Come up, Baldy! Come up, Baldy!" When he looked behind and saw them, he cursed the boys in the name of the Lord and then from the wildwood emerged two she-bears who tore apart forty-two of the children. From there, he headed to Mt. Carmel and afterward returned to Samaria (Kings 2, 23–25, my translation).

The crime hardly seems to matter—it's the sting of the slight that counts. Male pattern baldness is no less a reason to call on God's vengeance than the murder of your husband and son. What might seem to a bystander as the disproportionate use of force is for heaven to balance, not us poor mortals who might see such a scene as, well, overkill.

The word "wildwood" is most often translated as simply "woods" or "forest," but the notion of wildness needs to be stressed, I think. It's the notion of the heavens as elemental, the curse as an extension of nature, the wildness of a tornado or a hurricane or she-bears. The curse is the force of madness and rage, a different frequency from that of the supplicant murmuring gentle prayers. Curses are not sensible; they are not uttered in moments of reflection, and so the results can be messy.

Zora Neale Hurston records a curse from the Algiers section of New Orleans so long and mean that simply hearing it would have made me faint dead away:

"That the South wind shall scorch their bodies and make them wither and shall not be tempered to them," it reads in part. "That the North wind shall freeze their blood and numb their muscles and that it shall not be tempered to them. That the West wind shall blow away their life's breath and will not leave their hair grow, and that their fingernails shall fall off and their bones shall crumble. That the East wind shall make their minds grow dark, their sight shall fail and their seed dry up so that they shall not multiply." This is only a fraction of the text of the curse, which ends despairingly, "O Man God, I ask you for all these things because they have dragged me in the dust and destroyed my good name; broken my heart and caused me to curse the day I was born. So be it."

Despair and rage and dispossession find some solace in words and gestures toward an unseen hand that is much stronger than ours, and if it's not stronger or it refuses to slap silly our oppressors, then the words themselves have the power to make your blood pressure rise, whatever anger that lies inside you, rise volcanic to the surface. And that in itself is a partial remedy for impotent rage. The simple channeling of that anger into a funnel of spite. There's something undeniably beautiful about a well-worded curse.

In my own case, I put some curses on a group of summer campers in New Hampshire when I was eleven. I belonged at the time to an arcane secret society called "The Silver Sword Society." I was its only member and I have no idea how I came up with that name or the method of cursing people I didn't like—running them through with an invisible (but apparently silver) sword and then waiting for the curse to take effect. Every time I cursed someone, something bad happened almost immediately. I made one of my bunkmates so hysterical with my curses (after he'd dislocated a finger playing hot potato, something that could have been caused by nothing other than my curse, of course!), he, a hefty boy, sat on my chest until I agreed to remove the many swords with which I had impaled him. Later that day, I was visited by the head counselor Marty who solemnly warned me to "stop it already!" with the curses. I doubt he took the curses seriously, but he took the disruption of camp life quite seriously—drunk on my power, I had become a kind of curse kingpin in the days preceding his appeal to me, campers visiting me with requests in return for candy bars. Although my cursing days were over, I learned that the line of influence in this world is not always visible, rational, or wholly explicable. From my anthropology courses in my college career, I subsequently learned that in some societies, a curse is the only logical explanation for someone's misfortune.

In the several years since the woman in India cursed me, how has my life been affected? This is a tough question. My fortunes have not been terrible. A book I published that spring was met with good reviews but somewhat lackluster sales. A movie deal was struck and then fell through. I suffered a few colds, an inexplicable rash, a mild bout of depression. I was not rich yet and I was getting less handsome by the day. I believed that the old woman's magic was working. After learning that I had been cursed, a friend remarked, "Your life seems to be going pretty well."

"Ah, but how much better would my life be if I hadn't been cursed?"

This is a difficult question to answer, but one I determined to determine. While in Hong Kong, I asked my friend, the writer Xu Xi, a reasonable person, if she knew of anyone who might be able to remove a curse. I had known Xu Xi for fifteen years, but I never saw such a look on her face—she seemed to be reevaluating every moment of our long friendship. "A curse? No, I don't." And that was the end of that.

I finally had my chance when I brought a group of students to the Philippines and was making up the itinerary. I chose to visit Siquijor for a few days. Here, at last, was the opportunity to have my curse removed.

The healer we arranged to meet was a woman in her eighties who lived at the end of a dirt road in the hills of Siquijor. Her shack was a multi-purpose facility. Amid chickens and dogs, a few men sat around a videoke machine with large bottles of Red Horse beer. As I made my way across the courtyard, I banged my head smack into a post, probably not the most auspicious omen, but I tried to chalk it up to my clumsiness, rather than cosmic irony. On the other side of the ersatz karaoke bar was a small room that stank of ammonia from below the bamboo floor where the chickens used the chicken lavatory, but otherwise the room was neat if Spartan, its only decoration a calendar from Japan. From inside a dark room adjacent to the clinic wafted the sounds of the NBA playoffs, no more incongruous than the adjacent karaoke bar. The old woman, dressed rather stylishly in a purple blouse, her gray hair pulled back with a scrunchy into a ponytail, worked on a client, a woman suffering from asthma, while I waited on a bamboo bench and watched her work. With a wooden straw, she blew into a jar of clear water while moving the jar slowly around the woman's body, the sounds of the bubbles mixed with the old woman's grunts and sharp intakes of breath. There were no snakes, but it was still tactile and sensuous, and this is what you want when working with magic, to physicalize the mysterious and ineffable. Otherwise, how do you know it's working? A smooth stone lay at the bottom of the jar—the stone, she said, had been given to her by the Santo Niño. Her brand of magic was an amalgam of local animism and Catholicism; she crossed herself before she began her work. Of all Western religions, Catholicism is perhaps best suited to mix and match with other ancient rituals and beliefs, its pantheon of saints, its incense, its holy water, all tactile and visible manifestations of the mysterious at work in the world. Of all Western religions, few if any allow more for the intercession of the supernatural in the everyday lives of mortals. A friend of mine prays to St. Jude, the patron saint of lost causes, to find parking spaces, and she claims he always comes through for her. The trick of crossing your fingers for good luck originated in the Middle Ages as a quick sign of the cross to ward off the devil and evil spirits. Certainly, even the most skeptical among us, even my friend Xu Xi, have crossed our fingers.

As the woman blew on her straw, the water started growing cloudy and little specks of dirt floated in the jar. She stopped blowing and examined the jar, withdrew a piece of something and showed it to her patient, then rinsed the jar clean and filled it with water again, repeating the process of blowing into the water until it clouded again.

When it was my turn, my guide asked me what was wrong?

A curse, I said. A *barang*.

This was not her specialty, it turned out. She was better with asthma.

"What part of the body is affected?" she wanted to know.

That was hard to tell. "I don't know," I said. "Maybe the mind."

She nodded. "Fearful," she surmised.

She started in on me, blowing bubbles along my shoulder, my chest, my groin. My case was acute. I could have guessed as much. She used three jars of water on me, each one clouding up, big chunks of flotsam swirling in the water as she grunted and blew. Oddly, I didn't feel even slightly curious where the junk was coming from.

I should have been at least a tad curious. I'm related directly to Houdini. He was my great-grandmother's nephew. I suppose I was letting him down in my complete lack of interest in how the clear water became dirty. He spent much of his professional career debunking psychics, but only because he wanted so desperately to believe in an afterlife so that he could communicate with his departed mother. Psychics hated him and he was the object of many a curse. Who knows if they eventually worked? He did, after all, meet his end on Halloween.

I suppose a skeptic would assume the junk in the jar originated in the straw or that she hid it in her cheeks. Probably. Maybe. I don't know. I couldn't tell. At one point, she fished out a dark piece of something and said it looked like a scale of some sort. Before I could get too excited by the coincidence, I remembered that I had mentioned snakes when I was explaining the nature of my malady. She placed the dark thing on my finger and I studied it. Definitely not a scale but a soggy piece of wood. I passed it around the room, where some of my students were looking on. A few touched it, but most refused.

When the old woman had finished, she blew down my neck and said a prayer. I asked her if the curse was removed.

"*Wala*," she said. All gone.

Still, I bought a jar of special coconut oil from her, made with three hundred herbs, gathered during Holy Week and prepared on Black Saturday.

"And rituals," she said. "There are rituals for this."

Meanwhile, Margie was asking around for a *panangang* (protection) to counter the powerful spells of Evil Auntie Neneng that were killing or almost killing Margie's relatives. She wanted to find someone who specialized in barang, not asthma. Yes, there are such people, she was told, but they live high up in the mountains. They always do. I'm not sure why. But if you want someone powerful, don't expect to find her in a karaoke bar. You have to do some trekking. Unfortunately, we had limited time, so dispelling the spells of Evil Auntie Neneng would have to wait for another visit.

Of course, the question remains whether my curse was removed or not. I wondered in subsequent days whether an Indian curse could be removed by a Filipino healer who specializes in asthma. I even wondered whether I had indeed been cursed at all or if my woes, often indefinable, could be relegated to the nefarious and incurable human condition of daily life.

A couple of days later on the island of Bohol, while walking in my flip-flops on a side street, I severely gashed my big toe on a rock. Later that day, my eye inexplicably swelled shut. And that evening, while walking home from a bar on the beach, I gashed my other big toe open on another rock, this time so badly that my flip-flop was awash in blood and I left a rather ghastly trail all the way back to our hotel. I fretted that my curse seemed stronger than ever.

Six weeks later, I traveled to Cuba—that summer found me careening wildly from one point of the globe to the other, mostly for reasons to do with my teaching and writing. In Cuba, I was scouting a workshop of undergraduates I would lead later in the year. One of the stops on my itinerary that July was La Regla Church, one of the centers of Santeria belief in Cuba, and a short ferry ride across Havana's harbor. Of West African origin and hybridized by

Afro-Cuban slaves over several hundred years, Santeria is another manifestation of the dispossessed taking control of their lives in cosmic fashion, and another free mixing of Catholicism and animism. As my guide led me to the church, we passed a smattering of women seated on the curbside, calling to us to have our fortunes told. My guide, Yunelbis, a thirty-ish-year-old woman dressed smartly in her official guide shirt of light blue jeans and a pair of designer sunglass knockoffs, scoffed at one woman's entreaties to listen to her. "She may be a little mad," Yunie told me in English as the woman tried to tell her something that would make her pause and listen and linger and presumably pay.

I've seen many churches in my day—undoubtedly more churches than synagogues because churches are on any tour in nearly every land I have visited. La Regla Church itself was not the most impressive I've seen, but the fervor of the supplicants inside was more impressive than what I've witnessed under the echo-chamber domes of Europe's cathedrals, dozens of men and women praying passionately before icons, a hundred candles burning, each one a private supplication, human hope as always wafting upward to a vanishing point. The schlocky '70s tune "All by Myself" by Eric Carmen, piped in from overhead, competed with the sounds of prayer, dampening, for no one else but me, the solemnity of the collective supplication. Yunie pointed out the Santeras and Santeros, woman and men dressed all in white from head to toe—the religion had undergone a revival after originally being suppressed by the Communist Party. Now, even a number of the ruling elite are among believers in Santeria.

When we left the church, another woman seated on a low wall appealed for us to listen to her—Yunie had seemed so skeptical before that I assumed she would brush aside this woman as she had the first one, but she didn't. As if, well, in a spell, Yunie walked directly over to the woman and I followed. The woman, anywhere from forty to sixty years old, had a yellow kerchief tied around her hair and wore half a dozen bead necklaces, a couple of beaded bracelets, and jeans with chalk-like patterns that recalled, perhaps unintentionally, leg bones. Her name was Maritza, and she sat beside her own portable altar, at the center of which a most impressive doll resided. The doll's skin was dark like Maritza's and its lips were red and it wore glasses. Like Maritza, it too wore a kerchief, but one that was pointed in the back, somewhat more regal, like a pope's miter. Its ruffled yellow skirt was arrayed around it, and the doll, too, wore necklaces of beads. Her name was Francisca and she was the spirit with whom Maritza spoke in order to divine. Beside the doll stood a bottle of cacao oil on one side, and a statue of the Virgin Mary holding the Baby Jesus on the other.

I figured that it wouldn't hurt to get my curse removed again. Perhaps I would spend the rest of my life, traveling from one center of animism to another, trying to get my curse removed. This compulsion in itself might be a kind of curse. I told her through Yunie that I had been cursed by an old woman in India. "Yes," she said. "It's a powerful curse. Very powerful." I knew exactly what "very powerful" meant, and I took out my wallet.

She told me that I had stepped on something and that I was suffering health problems in my foot.

Upon reflection, it does seem to me now that the woman in India with the snakes cursed my feet. As I ran away from her in the market, she might logically (if logic has anything to do with it) curse the feet that were taking me away from her. Not only had I gashed both my toes on the same day, but recently I'd started to suffer from an intense pain in my left heel, a condition that has since been diagnosed by my doctor as Achilles tendonitis. I asked Maritza which foot was the one giving me problems. She brushed her hands along both legs, stood back and pointed decisively to my right foot. I couldn't be happier that she guessed wrong. If she had guessed correctly, I'd be a complete mess by now, instead of merely a partial mess.

We went ahead with the ritual. She tossed some cowrie shells. The shells landed right-side up and this, she said, meant I had the "blessing of Olofi," the Santeria name for the Almighty. She proceeded to rub cacao oil on my legs, told me to make the sign of the cross—hmm, not something I had much practice at. Mine was more like "the mark of Zorro." And she draped me with a white shell necklace and told me I needed to wear it always, but especially on Mondays and Fridays. Then she told me to give her some money and a *beso*, a kiss, on the cheek.

Intercession, of whatever variety, almost always feels good, whether it actually does good or not. While Christopher Hitchens, a devout atheist, expressly forbade Christians to pray for him when he was diagnosed with esophageal cancer, I say bring them on—the more prayers, the better. Send me your talismans too. I'm certain I've been cursed, as you undoubtedly have been cursed by someone somewhere at some time. Assume it's so and see if you can break the spell. My most recent foot ailment has practically healed though I don't wear my necklace very often, not even on Mondays and Fridays. I'd like to think at this point I'm curse-free, but I'll never know because it's just as difficult to tell whether you've been healed as whether you've been cursed.

Something Must Be Understood

Conventional wisdom holds that life is short, but a literary life, as it turns out, can be quite long. I don't think I appreciated this fully when, as a teenager, I first started seriously considering myself a writer. Back then, I never would have seen Sherwood Anderson as a model, a writer whose fame went through peaks and valleys throughout his lifetime, its zenith after the publication of his third book at the age of forty-three, *Winesburg, Ohio*. Certainly, Anderson was famous enough a writer to suit my adolescent vision of myself, but was he hip enough? When I wasn't daydreaming about my Nobel acceptance speech, I imagined myself the kind of writer who produces a few wild masterpieces and dies young and tragically. I wanted to be Rimbaud or Byron or Plath. It seemed to me no one could have much important to say after age forty. Sometimes, on my darkest days, now that I am well past my cutoff date, it still seems so.

Mention Sherwood Anderson these days, as I did recently at a dinner for a writer visiting my university, and it's as though you've mentioned something quaint and nostalgic, akin to the old Burma Shave ads along the roadside. Actually, my colleague to whom I had mentioned Anderson had a stronger reaction than that. Sherwood Anderson, he proclaimed, was a hack. To this, I responded that Sherwood Anderson certainly *wasn't* a hack, that in fact, he was a marvelous writer. To my relief, the visiting writer leaped to my defense, and more importantly, to Sherwood Anderson's. My colleague can be forgiven his disdain for Anderson because that's the way he is—a good man, but a man of brash, unreasoned assessments. Not only does he disdain Anderson, but he disdains all things Ohioan. Fortunately, Ohioans, like most Midwesterners, are not only accustomed to such irrational views, but take an almost perverse pleasure in how outré the rest of the country views them. In Walker Percy's *The Last Gentleman*, Percy's Mississippian protagonist jumps into a thorn bush in the snow simply to escape a group of overly friendly Ohioans with whom he's stranded at a ski lodge.

It's odd that Midwesterners are seen as overly friendly and vapid when, by and large, we're actually a rather dour and brooding lot. Even Midwesterners buy into such stereotypes of themselves. At the Illinois State Fair a number of years ago, I visited the Milk Tent, the mascot of which was an animatronic statue of Mark Twain, dressed in white and holding aloft a glass of milk, proclaiming how wholesome and refreshing milk is. Poor Mark Twain. This is the last activity he would have agreed to do in his lifetime. Sherwood Anderson, I believe, has suffered from a similar misreading and misremembering.

Anderson endured bouts of depression and self-doubt throughout much of his writing life. As with most writers, he was never satisfied with his sense of his own reputation. He could be unabashedly arrogant, proclaiming that he had written "one of the finest stories I've done, and I even dare say, one of the finest and most significant anyone has done." After entering into a short-sighted and hack-ish agreement to publish a novel a year for five years, one critic lamented: "The author of *Winesburg, Ohio* is dying before our eyes," and Hemingway and Fitzgerald proclaimed that Anderson's career as a writer was over. Yet, it was far from over, and his disappointments simply seasoned him and brought an added complexity to his work. "A man has to begin over and over," he wrote to a friend in 1939. In such a career, I find a philosophical comfort. For me, dreams of being Plath, Rimbaud, or Byron are distant memories. I see instead that worrying about one's place in the pantheon of writers not only gets in the way of living but writing as well. It's not only Anderson's life as a writer that has informed my own, but his stories, and one in particular.

I don't remember exactly how or when I first ran across Anderson's "Death in the Woods," but it's a story that has influenced me greatly in my approach to fiction and nonfiction both. This later work of Anderson's is either a story disguised as a memoir or a memoir disguised as a story, or perhaps both.

In the story, a narrator attempts to reconstruct an episode from his youth in which a woman was found frozen to death between the town and the farm on which she lived. From the first line, we know that this is a story that has the act of remembering at its core: "She was an old woman and lived on a farm near the town in which I lived." As this is a short story and Anderson is a writer firmly rooted within the realist camp, we recognize this first line as an attempt by the author to lend an air of verisimilitude by introducing the device of a narrator remembering something from his youth as though he were writing a conventional memoir. But with Anderson, it's more than a device. Many of his stories were based on his youth, and often he did little to disguise fact as fiction. As a boy, Anderson worked as a groom or "swipe" in a livery stable, and some of his most famous stories, such as "I Am a Fool," have the racing circuit or livery as their backdrop. In the summer of 1895, Anderson worked for a man named Tom Whitehead who is mentioned in "Death in the Woods" without disguise, and is only minimally disguised in "I Am a Fool" and "An Ohio Pagan" as Harry Whitehead. Why the attempt at all when it's such a flimsy one, except that perhaps this isn't an attempt to cover up as much as it is to subtly cue the author's own imagination, to give Anderson permission to invent as he remembers? As Anderson wrote, "While art is distinct from real life, the imagination must constantly feed upon reality or starve."

The first page or so of the story classifies the old woman as a type of person familiar to rural towns, the type of woman one sees coming and going to market, but whose name one never really knows or cares to know. We see her in passing, wearily bearing her burdens on the roadside. She is the epitome of one unloved and neglected by society. But Anderson goes on to particularize this woman, telling us the circumstances of her hard life and background. First, he pauses again in the narrative to reinforce the notion that this story is an act of memory: "I have just suddenly now remembered her and what happened. It is a story." And a little further on he states, "It all comes back clearly now."

I love that simple line, "It is a story," so pedestrian and matter of fact one could easily miss it. I take it to mean that it's a full-formed narrative within the narrator's mind. Or perhaps it's a kind of stunned realization: "I have just suddenly now . . . remembered. It is a story." Whether remembered or not, the narrator (and perhaps Anderson) is reminding himself and us that the story (that is, the way in which events are ordered) takes precedence over memory, not the other way around.

The narrator then proceeds to recount what he knows of the old woman's life. An orphan, she'd been "bound" to a German farmer who tried to force himself on her. His wife, suspecting the farmer's attraction, treated her miserably as well. She was rescued from this life by a man named Jake Grimes, himself a hard-bitten and habitually criminal sort. She and Grimes had two children, a daughter who died and a son who grew up as tough and loveless as his father. Such was her lot, but she didn't complain, resigned as she was to her role in life as little more than someone enslaved.

It is a story. And as such, Anderson has the liberty to delve into the psyche of the old woman, which he does for the better part of the narrative. Her main concern in life, it seems, is how to contrive to feed all the things in her care. There are her husband and son, the husband's pack of dogs, the farm animals. . . .

One winter's day, she treks into town to trade some eggs, and on the return trip she rests in the snow beside a tree and freezes to death. Her husband's dogs, which have followed her, circle her body and finally tear at her pack where her provisions are stored. In the process, her clothes are torn from her body clear to the hips.

Anderson writes: "Such things happened in towns of the Middle West, on farms near town, when I was a boy. A hunter after rabbits found the old woman's body and did not touch it. . . . I was in Main Street with one of my brothers who was the town newsboy."

Realist stories, almost by definition, try to make the reader forget the story is artificial. The realist writer wants to create a kind of transparency that allows the reader to vicariously experience "real life" through the characters of the story. Anderson could have maintained this sense of transparency if the story were simply about the death of a pathetic old woman. Such a story would have little impact except that it would make us shake our heads and say, "Gee, life is tough," as though we didn't already know that. But this is a story about observation, a story about the observer trying to understand what it's like to be another person, an impossible necessity.

Memoirists have the same aim as the realist writer. They try to make the reader forget the story is artificial and that memory is fallible. If Anderson were alive today and presented this story as nonfiction rather than fiction, or as the combination known as "autofiction," we might even put aside assigning it a genre.

The "I" of the story recounts how he and his brother tagged along with the men of the town and how he'd seen the body of the frail woman lying in the snow, and the impact it made upon him.

"I had seen everything," Anderson writes, "had seen the oval in the snow, like a miniature race track, where the dogs had run, had seen how the men were mystified, had seen the white bare young-looking shoulders, had heard the whispered comments of the men. . . . Later, in town, I must have heard other fragments of the old woman's story."

As though fascinated and mesmerized by the memory of the woman's body in the snow, the narrator once again recounts the picture frozen in his mind: "I remember only the picture there in the forest, the men standing about, the naked girlish-looking figure face down in the snow, the tracks made by the running dogs and the clear cold winter sky above . . ."

When we finish a realist piece of fiction, we don't conclude, unless we're naive, "What an amazing true story!" We realize the boundaries of the genre, that we're reading something contrived, no matter how much it might be based on real life. A story is not meant to be a factual account. But Anderson turns the last section of the story into an account of how the story came to be.

Here, if you'll indulge me, I need to quote a substantial bit of text from the story in order to get my point across. Anderson writes:

The scene in the forest had become for me, without my knowing it, the foundation for the real story I am now trying to tell. The fragments, you see, had to be picked up slowly, long afterwards.

Things happened. When I was a young man I worked on the farm of a German. The hired girl was afraid of her employer. The farmer's wife hated her.

I saw things at that place. Once later, I had a half-uncanny, mystical adventure with dogs in an Illinois forest on a clear, moonlit winter night. When I was a schoolboy, and on a summer day, I went with a boy friend out along a creek some miles from town and came to the house where the old woman had lived. No one had lived in the house since her death. The doors were broken from the hinges; the window lights were all broken. As the boy and I stood in the road outside, two dogs, just roving farm dogs no doubt, came running around the corner of the house. The dogs were tall, gaunt fellows and came down to the fence and glared through at us, standing in the road.

The whole thing, the story of the old woman's death, was to me as I grew older like music heard from far off. The notes had to be picked up slowly one at a time. Something had to be understood. . . .

You see it is likely that, when my brother told the story that night when we got home and my mother and sister sat listening, I did not think he got the point. He was too young and so was I. A thing so complete has its own beauty.

I shall try not to emphasize the point. I am only explaining why I was dissatisfied then and have been ever since. I speak of that only that you may understand why I have been impelled to tell the simple story over again.

And so the story ends.

To me, the self-consciousness of the narrator in "Death in the Woods" is what makes the story so brilliant—it is both a simple story as Anderson claims and a complex one. It has taken the narrator/Anderson the better part of his life to understand that the story is not solely about the old woman, but about the reaction to the old woman's death, the spectacle of it, and the memory of it. Something must be understood.

We remember only fragments, and the fragments present themselves as crystalline notes within our minds, but not stories. Fascinated by the music recalled, we trouble it in memory, we marvel at its mysterious persistence. If only we could remember, we might also figure out something crucial about our own lives. Sometimes, as Anderson shows us, we can get within earshot of, if not understanding, then at least appreciating the simplicity and beauty of those far-off notes.

Skinny Dipping with James Agee

Ever since I was sixteen, and attended tiny St. Andrew's School, nestled in the mountains of Tennessee, one of the same schools James Agee attended (along with Exeter and Harvard), I've seen him as a kind of role model, both for good and ill. My role models have always looked nothing like me and have tempted me with their wicked ways, both linguistically and temperamentally. In grad school (I first wrote "grand" school), when I was a "gradual student," (to quote John Irving), I identified with my teacher and sometime downstairs neighbor, Barry Hannah. In high school, it was James Agee, in whose eponymous library on the campus of St. Andrew's you could find me studying under the not-so-watchful eye of the librarian, Mrs. Gooch. Unlike most of my fellow St. Andrewsians, I lived for study hall, and I immersed myself in southern literature full of madness and disgrace. As in the children's story in which an alligator is raised by ducks and thinks he's a duck too, I disregarded the fact that my background had little in common with possessed southerners like Hannah and Agee.

I had *something* in common with Agee, besides going to St. Andrew's and sitting through Anglican chapel services. Agee and I had both lost our fathers when we were young, his when he was six and mine when I was seven. But that wasn't what forged my connection with him. By the time I graduated from St. Andrew's, I had read almost nothing of James Agee's work. Why would a school that prided itself in forging young Jim's character overlook his writing? I wondered. The only Agee texts that were pushed on me—I can't speak for other St. Andrewsians of the time—were the letters of James Agee to Father Flye, a former teacher at St. Andrew's who lived past one hundred to Agee's forty-five, dead of a heart attack in Manhattan in the back seat of a cab on his way to see a doctor. Not that Agee's work was discouraged at St. Andrew's—I remember seeing Agee's autobiographical novel *A Death in the Family* on the shelves of the library. I might have even picked it up. I might have even stolen it to read later.

But Agee wasn't really southern literature as defined by St. Andrew's at the time. When I took Mr. Norton's Southern Literature class, we read four Faulkner novels. Couldn't one of Agee's books have supplanted one of the Faulkner's? After all, one of Agee's works, *The Morning Watch*, took place at a thinly veiled St. Andrew's, for Heaven's sake. Mr. Norton, whose great-grandfather survived two horses shot from under him when he was defending against the Northern Aggressors, didn't seem to care for any Black writers either. He decidedly preferred the old South to the new, even assigning us a book about "Quadroons and Octaroons," *The Grandissimes: A Story of Creole Life*, written by George Washington Cable in 1880. For Mr. Norton, Southern Literature meant White Literature, not that this was ever explicitly stated. It didn't need stating. I don't think he particularly considered a Yankee Jew as the ideal student for his class either. Too late now for me to turn in a negative teacher evaluation for Mr. Norton—not that we were ever asked to fill out such things, but the *Grandissimes* I could have lived without. Agee, on the other hand . . . I'm not sure if it would have helped me or hurt me to read *Let Us Now Praise Famous Men* at the age of sixteen. It probably would have confounded and devastated and frustrated and sometimes bored me as it has since I first discovered it years later.

We're all ruins in the making, and that's what I love so much about Agee, that he was a ruin on the page. When he ventured in 1936 with Walker Evans down to Alabama for Henry Luce's *Fortune* Magazine, he met three white tenant farm families, forming a kind of ruinous circle of human enterprise and squalor that he found himself in for several weeks, and that he tried, in vain (he thought), to capture these people in his writing on the page. He wrote:

> If I could do it, I'd do no writing at all here. It would be photographs; the rest would be fragments of cloth, bits of cotton, lumps of earth, records of speech, pieces of wood and iron, phials of odor, plates of food and of

excrement. Booksellers would consider it quite a novelty; critics would murmur, yes, but is it art; and I could trust the majority of you to use it as you would a parlor game.

A piece of the body torn out by the roots might be more to the point. As it is, though, I'll do what little I can in writing.

In an introduction to the work of Argentine novelist Macedonio Fernández, novelist Adam Thirlwell writes that it's long been a wish of the avant-garde "to make a novel which is in fact a reality: that art only has a value in so far as it stops being art." I'm not sure that I'd classify Agee as avant-garde, but I believe this is what he was after, this impossible desire to give us not an ordinary book but a body. Walker Evans called Agee's delirious and doomed attempt to accomplish this, "night writing," a work that could only be written by a twenty-seven-year-old who takes himself seriously to the point of pomposity. Still, I love all the flaws of this great ruin of a book. In it, I see all our failures to capture what we want to capture, yours and mine. I've passed the time when I could conceivably write such a majestic failure. I'm out of "grand" school though still a "gradual student," which means my failures have become increasingly fatal, like a slow carbon monoxide leak.

Had Mr. Norton made us read James Agee, I'm not sure how I would have reacted, but I would have reacted. *The Grandissimes* still sits in me, undigestible.

I only truly discovered Agee after high school when I first read his gorgeous evocation of place, "Knoxville, Summer 1915," followed by *A Death in the Family*, the copy I stole when Mrs. Gooch wasn't looking, and *The Morning Watch*. But first, I acted out *The Morning Watch*. Although I wasn't taught Agee's work, I was taught some good old-fashioned southern self-destructiveness at St. Andrew's: a little drunkenness, a little weed, a lot of pining for sex, and even more conflict about religion. Jew or not, I had to participate in the high Anglican rituals of the campus along with all the other Agee wannabes. All students were required on the eve of Easter Sunday to participate in "Morning Watch," a kind of relay prayer in which we were required to pray alone to Jesus in the chapel for fifteen minutes before being relieved by another student. My watch came at 3:00 a.m., an hour before Agee's slot in his time. This was punishment, I'm sure, for being a Jew from New York City, punishment for getting the award from Mr. Norton for best student in his Southern Literature class ("It pains me to give you this award, Mr. Hemley," he told me when I went to receive it on the St. Andrew's stage that May). What was I supposed to say to Jesus? Agee suffered spiritual torment during his own stint with Jesus during Morning Watch. For me, there was only resentment at having been awakened so early for something I didn't believe in. But there came a reward. One of the girls I had a crush on—none of the girls were crush-exempted, actually—suggested that we do what the main characters in *The Morning Watch* did in Agee's book: ride our bikes out to the lake and go skinny-dipping. She didn't have to ask twice. Half a dozen of us Agee heathens rode our bikes out to the lake and luxuriated in the warmth and freedom of being sixteen and not on the downhill slide. And from that moment, throwing off my clothes, when I hit the water, skinny bones and all, that's the time I mark as when I first understood something about literature.

The Hypocrite's Guide to Saving the Earth

"You can see the clubhouse at Timberland Heights from here," Margie's Auntie Lillian says on a visit one afternoon, pointing out the window of our condo at the mountains in the distance. "They always ask me to bring people there. They think, because I'm a doctor, I'm rich. But we can just visit sometime and make *pasyal*, if you like."

I always like to make pasyal—it's probably what I do best: roam around and have fun. A clubhouse in a wealthy enclave. I can deal. And besides, I'd never say no to Auntie Lillian or any of my in-laws.

The following Saturday, we're met by Auntie Lillian, in the company of a Mrs. Laredo of Timberland Heights. Margie and I sit in the backseat while Auntie Lillian, Mrs. Laredo, and the driver sit up front. Forty-five minutes later, we're waved through the grand entrance to Timberland Heights by a guard in a booth. "See how close it is to the city?" Mrs. Laredo gushes. But what distinguishes Timberland Heights from any other development, says Mrs. Laredo, is how eco-friendly it is. Some of the lots are even classified as farms—organic, of course. On these lots, you can only build on 20 percent of the land. Forty-four percent of the community, in fact, has been designated as farmland.

I could imagine myself living here, I think, as we walk toward a cliff occupied for the present by trees and knee-high grass. A water tower rises in the near distance, but that's the only obstruction except for the trees. "Once you clear the trees," Mrs. Laredo tells me, "you'll be able to see the view."

"How much is a lot?" I ask when I step back in the car.

Eight-point-nine million pesos, or about $190,000, but that's for the rock-bottom-cheapest lot, and that's without the house, and no farm—hardly even any land between your lot and the neighbor's.

Up, up, up we climb, on roads three hundred fifty meters (about 1,150 feet) above sea level. "Look at that view, sir!" Mrs. Laredo tells me. We climb toward the fabled clubhouse, a glinting structure as big as an oil tanker. How could I have missed such a behemoth when Lillian pointed it out last week?

As we're climbing, Margie and I notice that some of the property markers seem to designate sheer cliff sides fronting the road. "How do you build on a cliff?" I ask Mrs. Laredo.

She hooks an arm over the front seat and flashes us a smile. "Oh, that's not your problem. That's a problem for the architect," she says.

"What about earthquakes?" Margie asks.

Mrs. Laredo shrugs. "We're one and a half kilometers from the fault line," she tells us.

Margie gives a little cough/laugh at that and we exchange looks of disbelief. Well, yes, I guess tumbling off a cliff could be considered eco-friendly as long as the building materials were biodegradable. People certainly are.

Mrs. Laredo spots one of her customers, Dr. Lucinda, surveying his farm lot. A lot of *Balikbayans* (returning Filipinos) live here, she explains, waving to the good doctor, a balding man in his fifties sitting in a *bahay kubo* (a native-style hut) on his farm property. One Australian bought eight lots for 50 million pesos, or a million dollars and some change. The doctor likes the development so much that when he bought a lot with a house for 10.2 million, he also bought the lot next door, as well as the lot in front, so that his view wouldn't be obstructed. We park in the doctor's driveway and are met by his wife, their son, and the son's girlfriend, a woman in her early thirties dressed in a leotard. The son has just purchased an apartment in Hell's Kitchen, in Manhattan—so little space, he tells me, and look at what you can get here for that much. He goes off to play Frisbee with his girlfriend in the extra lot his dad purchased for 9 million.

Mrs. Laredo appears on cue at my elbow. "Look at that view, sir!"

She takes us across the street to the shell of a house, which can be completed to our specifications . . . if we hurry!

As we tour the half-finished house, I notice, a little down the road, a circle with a big H in the middle. "I was looking for somewhere to park my helicopter," I tell Mrs. Laredo.

Mrs. Laredo tells me that at least four congressmen live here. "We have to be discreet," she says. "We can't say who they are. Unexplained wealth."

An "African Jew," she says, is the biggest investor in Timberland Estates— he's invested billions. But, again, she won't tell me his name.

We get back in the car and climb further to the clubhouse. "If you buy a farm," Mrs. Laredo explains, "membership in the clubhouse is free. Otherwise, it's 580,000 pesos."

"And look at that view, sir!" she says.

My God! I haven't seen that view for thirty seconds at least.

In a couple of years, a sign as big as the Hollywood sign will lead people to Timberland Heights. "You'll be able to see it from anywhere in Manila," Mrs. Laredo brags. "If you're lost, you can just point to the sign and say, 'That's where I live!'"

But the sign is hardly needed. The clubhouse of Timberland Heights sits as big as Chernobyl on the hill, five stories high, housing an infinity pool, a bowling alley, a karaoke lounge, a beauty parlor, a basketball court, a handball court, and chandeliers as big as water buffalo. Soon, a shopping mall, a five-star hotel, and an international school will rise behind the clubhouse, further serving the residents of Timberland Heights in their pursuit of self-sufficiency, clean air, and the simple country life.

Bodyguards must wait outside, which isn't a problem for me (yet), but I *am* outraged that there's no jai-alai court, and I ask Mrs. Laredo, why the oversight?

Margie tells me to be quiet, though she laughs. "Honey, they won't appreciate your sense of humor," she tells me.

Then we leave the clubhouse and descend the mountain to the base of Timberland Heights, where Mrs. Laredo wants to show us the butterfly house and the organic gardens.

"It's too bad you missed the farmers' market this morning," she tells me, "because the owners were selling their organic produce." For a second, I envision the good doctor, his son, and the leotard-clad girlfriend hawking eggplants under the hot sun, but then I turn to Margie.

"The owners don't sell their produce, do they?" I say. "The servants do."

"Of course," she says, as though I just don't get it.

In the clubhouse, a scale model of Timberland Heights is kept like the Ark of the Covenant. "Maybe I can afford the scale model," I say, and Margie shoots me a look. A poster beside the scale model proudly proclaims Timberland Height's raison d'être:

> *The encroachment of progress has laid siege upon our natural resources and it is up to us to take responsibility for the land. We intend to realize this vision of ecological responsibility at Timberland Heights, a natural living sanctuary where men and nature could harmoniously exist side-by-side. By designing a community that blends in and enhances the lay of the land, we create a viable haven for generations to come.*

I've read some fine bullshit over the years, but this is the richest. One word of this credo could fertilize an organic farm for a year.

Mrs. Laredo hands us off to a middle-aged man wearing a U.S. Embassy T-shirt, who takes us to a picnic table and tells us of more of Timberland Heights's wonders: a twenty-four-kilometer nature trail, three waterfalls, and ten thousand trees that have been planted. Where? I wonder. All I saw were hectares of denuded hillsides. Perhaps they planted them in the scale model?

This is a great time to buy, because of the economic crisis, he tells me as we eat glow-in-the-dark macaroni salad. Once the crisis is over, it won't be so good anymore. Ninety-five percent of Mandala One (the farmland) has been sold and only 30 percent of Mandala Two remains. It's here I point out to the man that I am a foreigner and so cannot by law own any portion of Mandala One or Two—and even though I trust Margie (though not quite so much after this escapade), I'd want my name on any property I bought.

Sad, sad, sad, that I cannot be part of this grand environmental endeavor after all. As we drive away, I take one last look at the clubhouse. Outside the gates, there's something comforting in the familiar sights: shanties, people burning garbage by the side of the road, a man peeing on a wall unabashedly.

The Air Supply Guide to Matrimonial Bliss

She of the Karaoke Tribe, from the Archipelago of the Interminable Love Song, where Karen Carpenter never goes out of style, has not asked me to prove my love, but when she says she wants to go with her Filipina émigré friends to Diamond Jo Casino in Dubuque, Iowa, to see Air Supply Live! in concert, I seize this as an opportunity, after twelve years of marriage, akin to a renewal of vows, and as close to sacrificing my life for her as I'm going to get. It's a "get out of jail free" card, and one I will hold in reserve. "Yes, I cheated on you with your best friend, but don't forget, I went to see Air Supply Live! with you at Diamond Jo Casino in Dubuque."

Hard work, marriage.

You remember Air Supply and what they sang. Of course you do. That song. And the one that sounded just like it, and that other one too. Yeah. Those.

If I seem as enthusiastic about the concert as a zombie at a baby shower, then that's twice as enthusiastic as I mean to seem. I embarrass easily. I'm overly self-conscious, and when someone does something really stupid around me, such as wearing a fake deer head to get attention, as I saw recently on a commuter flight, I feel that it's me wearing that deer head. The same holds true at an Air Supply concert. I feel as though it's me belting out stale lyrics along with the audience.

But it's not me. It's Margie. She is a loyal soul who loves without apology or embarrassment. I did not grow up listening to Air Supply, and so I don't see what she sees performing onstage. I see a man, bedecked with a rhombus of white hair and a tag-sale Sgt. Pepper jacket, and his taller partner, Russell, likewise white-haired, with a microphone wrapped from ear to mouth. The room, including the stage and bar, is only about half the size of an Olympic swimming pool. Does Russell need a microphone at all?

"It's great to be back in your lovely state," Russell tells the crowd of a hundred and fifty at most. Margie and I sit in folding chairs near the front of the stage. "Everyone says that, don't they?"

And it's true that it feels like a line, but he has to say it, I guess. It's part of the package, though he conspicuously left off the name of the state it's so great to be back in. Is he thinking, *Idaho? No, Ohio? I had it a second ago!*

Guitar strung around his neck, he tries to make a connection with the chattering crowd. "Do you ever feel you need to go someplace alone?" he asks. "I need that. In my house, I have places that no one knows about . . . not even me. A sanctuary." He laughs and turns to the band of four young men behind him, who seem awake enough to give him courtesy laughs in return.

I do like his sense of irony. He has my respect for that. Maybe he couldn't care less about this quadrillionth gig of his, but he has to pretend he cares, while dropping hints that he's not going to take himself too seriously anymore.

The other one, Graham, keeps signaling for more applause, talks about this being the kickoff of the world tour. "Can you rock it for me?" he asks.

The people beside Margie can't rock it for him or anyone, nodding slightly as though sitting on the tarmac waiting for their plane to be de-iced, and Margie asks to change places with me.

Graham has noticed three empty seats in the front row. Empty seats bother him and he wants them filled immediately. Did they leave? Were they never filled? Margie's Filipina friends, closer to the stage than she, dash to fill them.

"I don't believe we fall in love," Russell says, as smoke billows. "I believe love falls into us. Write that down, guys."

"Is he Shakespeare?" someone near me asks. The audience is not full of dewy teens. They've been through it all, and so they joke about how incredibly large that woman is—the one who's Every Woman in the World. They want to drink a beer, maybe play the slots. It's an alliance between half the audience and Big Russell, the ironist. The other half of the audience, which includes Margie and her Filipina friends, are in alliance with Graham. They believe that love has fallen into them, that love will lift them up on stage.

Graham and Russell cycle through their hits, which, now that they're singing them, are familiar even to me. "You Are My Lady," "Lost in Love," and then Russell sings a new composition called "Everywhere," the basic idea of which seems to be that someone (you) is everywhere. Everywhere the singer goes. Everywhere the singer imagines. In his heart and most likely in his soul, although his soul isn't explicitly mentioned in the lyrics.

He confides in the way that someone confides in a bunch of people one doesn't know that he likes to sit on the porch and look at the mountains. Wait for something to happen. If something doesn't happen he drinks a bottle of wine. Then something happens.

Next song, he drops into the audience like a paratrooper with a shattered knee. "He's everywhere," a wag behind me says. But he's singing one of his big hits. I know he is, though I have no idea what it's called. It's that big one. That big hit. Like the other ones. Not like "Everywhere," which has as much of a chance of becoming a hit now as "The Farmer in the Dell." But for him, his career marches on. There's nothing stopping him, not even advancing age. I ask Margie the name of the song. She's waving to him. She's been waving to him the entire concert. "You're Every Woman in the World to Me," she rattles off.

"Again?" I ask.

"No," she says, acknowledging her mistake, but also acknowledging that I'm a pest by waving her hand at me, not in the same way she waves it at Big Russell.

It's "Here I Am!" which sounds kind of like Every Other Song in the World to Me.

Oh my! Graham is wading into the audience too, and has kissed a woman full on the lips. Get out the nitro tablets. He leads the audience in an a cappella version of "Here I Am." The concert is going karaoke. Someone ululates. Do people ululate at Air Supply concerts? The lighters come out, both real and virtual.

In the afterglow of the concert, Margie shyly asks if I'd mind waiting while she stands in line for an Air Supply T-shirt. The shirt costs forty-five dollars. But, on the bright side, you get a CD of their new music, which presumably includes "Everywhere" and "Everything," and maybe even "Everybody" and "You Are My Lost in Love Lady/Woman and Here I Am to Me."

"Sure," I say, "Go ahead. I'll play the slots." And I say it without any sense of irony or cynicism. I mean, she *is* my lady. While she's standing in line for the ephemera so meaningful to her, to have it signed, to look into their eyes and see a connection, I put five dollars in one of the penny slots in the casino twice the size of the performance area, and I start to hum "All Out of Love" because there's a part of my brain that, despite all the other parts, is sentimental and earnest and believes that all you have to do is believe. It's not love that falls into me, but money from this slot machine. Within minutes, I've won nearly three hundred dollars, more than enough to repay myself for the tickets, for dinner, for the gas, for her exorbitant T-shirt. When Margie comes by to collect me, I belt out a bar of one of Air Supply's famous songs, hoping she believes it's true.

How to Change History, Redux

In some ways, driving every day to De La Salle University doesn't make a whole lot of sense, though in other ways it does. An hour's commute from my condo in the morning, using shortcuts and side roads to avoid the traffic, my little office within the grounds of the university is a haven. I love my family, but the condo is small and my study is also Shoshie's bedroom. She bursts in at least six times a morning looking for a toy, and if I lock the door, she just pounds on it, yelling, "Daddy, I'll be quiet!" And then there's one-and-a-half-year-old Naomi screaming a mixed Tagalog/English/Gibberish version of "You Raise Me Up" at the top of her lungs on the other side of the door, and Margie in the living room playing music, and well, what's an hour's commute in the grand scheme of things? When my friend, the writer Dinah Roma, who runs the Bienvenido Santos Center at DLS, offered me a little writing office at the center, I did everything but fall prostrate at her feet.

I've come to enjoy the commute. Along the way, I people watch and building watch and practice my Tagalog on Rey as we drive across the Pasig River, its polluted waters clogged with vegetation, a sign bedecking a bridge reading, "Save the River of our Dreams"; or past the facade of a once-grand railway station, in limbo between destruction and neglect, or the race track in Santa Ana that is no longer used. Or the ramshackle ancient houses nearly caving in, with their Capiz shell windows.

I play a game as I travel. What did Manila look like a hundred years ago? Or seventy, back when it was known (along with about every other Asian city, it seems) as "The Pearl of the Orient"? But this game is a melancholic one, and when I tire of it, I ask my driver (which sounds so grand. What he drives is a little green Isuzu Fuego pickup truck on loan from my brother-in-law, not a Mercedes, though it has a laughably important little sign attached to the front that reads, "Doctor on Board. Do Not Delay!") to buy a newspaper from a hawker at the next light or traffic jam so I can catch up on the latest bit of scandal. Gossip and scandal here almost always trump history.

One day, as we're headed home I'm struck by something I almost never see in Manila, a shiny historical marker in the middle of a small bridge. The bridge is in disrepair, shanties lining the river beside it, part of its cement wall breached as though a car drove through. Although the marker is in a spot that makes it difficult to read, I ask Rey to pull over.

"Where are we, Rey?"

"This is the San Juan Bridge."

Oh, I have stumbled on some history. This is where popular legend has it that the Philippine-American War started in 1899 when a soldier from the Nebraska Volunteers fired on a Filipino sentry. Actually, the shots were fired elsewhere in Santa Mesa, but I'd like to see what the historical marker says. Alas, it's in Tagalog and I'm afraid that my Tagalog isn't good enough to decipher it all. About all I can make out are the words "Nebraska Volunteers."

Until I first arrived in the Philippines in 1999, I, like so many Americans, had only the foggiest notion that there had ever been such a thing as a war between the Philippines and the United States. It barely even registered that the Philippines had once been a colony of ours after we defeated them in their bid for freedom that our history books referred to (if at all) as the Philippine Insurrection. I occasionally run into otherwise intelligent Americans who, to this day, ask me if we still "own" the Philippines. Although the question never fails to shock me, I know there are some Filipinos who would answer a sardonic "yes."

I ask Rey if he will please read the sign for me and tell me what it says.

"I think it's about the Japanese," he says, peering at the sign through the windshield.

"I kind of doubt that," I say. "This isn't a World War II site."

He's silent for a bit. "There was fighting here, sir," he says. And then a moment later he practically jumps out of his seat. "Oh! The Filipinos and the Americans were fighting?!" He turns to me, his face registering both concern and surprise.

"Yes," I tell him, "but it was a long time ago." And I give him a quick history of the conflict as we proceed home. Of course, I feel awkward and uncomfortable telling a Filipino about his own history, and I don't want to seem at all condescending toward him. But I've studied Filipino history extensively over the years, starting with my research for a book on the Philippines I published in 2003. In any case, it's not *that* unusual for a working-class Filipino to be oblivious to much of his country's history. Many Americans are ignorant of America's history. Why should it be different here?

Rey is silent, mulling it over. I'm looking at the shanties and trying to imagine what this place looked like during the war. I imagine there was little but this bridge here. This was the countryside. Now it's a jam-packed detour beside a murky river.

"But I thought the Americans and the Filipinos fought the Japanese together," he says finally.

"They did," I say. "That was later, in World War II."

He tells me he thinks there's a tunnel nearby where the Japanese hid. It's called *Pinaglabanan*, which means "Fighting." So we make a short detour to see the place. It's now some kind of park. A sign reads: MUSEO KATIPUNAN.

The Katipunan were the group of Filipino patriots who plotted the ouster of the Spanish who had been their colonial masters for over three hundred years. This is the site, I learn later, of the first battle of the Philippine Revolution—a battle in 1896 in which the Filipinos, outgunned by the Spanish, were fairly slaughtered. But I mistakenly tell Rey that I think the site has to do with more fighting between the Filipinos and Americans. Not the Japanese, though for all I know there might well be a tunnel there where the Japanese once hid.

"Why did the Japanese want the Philippines?" Rey asks.

"First, the Spanish came," I tell him, "They wanted to conquer the world."

"Like Hitler?" he asks.

"No, not Hitler," I say, "You know, they ruled the Philippines for almost four hundred years, and then the Filipinos had them cornered in Intramuros ..."

"Magellan?" he asks.

"No, not Magellan."

During the Spanish-American War, I tell him, the Filipinos and Americans were allies. The Filipinos thought they were going to get independence, but America decided to buy the Philippines from the Spanish, even though Filipinos didn't want to be bought. "The Filipinos knew they couldn't beat the Americans, but they fought anyway because they were willing to die for their independence," I say. It's silly, I know, but at the word, "independence," I tear up a little bit. There's hardly a word in the American lexicon more sacred than that—it's the irony that gets me, I guess. But I quickly recover. "The Philippines lost and was a colony of the U.S. for fifty years. Until the Japanese came and fought . . ."

Here, Rey interrupts me. "And it was called 'The Longest Day.'"

"No, that was in Europe," I say. "That was 'D-day.'"

"And many Americans died here on 'The Longest Day.'"

I give up. "Yes, that's right," I say. What does it matter anyway? My condo building is in sight.

"The best movie I watch, sir," says Rey, warming up to our history lesson, "is between America and Vietnam, sir. *Full Metal Jacket.* I love watching war, sir."

I sit back in my seat as Rey segues seamlessly into a litany of the grossest foods he's ever eaten, the friendship between our two countries restored, the world's equilibrium intact.

The Writer across the Table

I sat near the front window of a coffeehouse I frequented called the Runcible Spoon, reading a book by my favorite author, the Argentinean Jorge Luis Borges. *Labyrinths*. Perhaps this was my third time through the book. The story I was currently rereading, "Pierre Menard, Author of the Quixote" involved an author whose life project was to write a book that had already been written, *Don Quixote*. The story, like so many of Borges's, involved conundrums and puzzles, and was loosely based on the paradox of an infinite number of monkeys banging away on an infinite number of typewriters for an infinite number of hours. Eventually, the idea went, the monkeys would write all the great works of literature. Pierre Menard, monkey-like, wanted to write *Don Quixote*. Not rewrite it or copy it but write it as Pierre Menard. But in his lifetime, he was only able to write one chapter of the classic. The narrator of the story, a friend of Menard's, compares in a perfect deadpan two paragraphs from the original Quixote and Menard's Quixote. Of course, they're identical, but at the same time they're not because one was written by a seventeenth-century Spaniard and the other was written by someone from the vantage point of the twentieth century. In other words, the intervening four hundred years of history colors the writers' perceptions, creates an ironic distance, grants knowledge of the world and its peoples and its literatures that the original author never could have imagined. Your Quixote will be different from my Quixote, though they might have the exact words in the same order. Like so many of Borges's stories, it was brilliant—not only was it clever and funny, but it showed how every act of writing is at once both imitation and wholly original, and how imperfect the act of communication is between reader and writer.

As I read and savored the story, I became vaguely aware of a commotion near me. A small crowd had gathered near the window and door of the coffeehouse, and they were buzzing about something. I looked up at the server near me as she craned her head to get a peek out the window closest to me.

"What's going on?" I asked.

"It's Borges, of course," she said, as though Borges always came into the Runcible Spoon. Indeed, Borges was walking slowly up the path to the coffeehouse, led carefully by a young woman.

This meeting was not quite the heavy-handed coincidence it might seem at first glance. Yes, I was reading Borges's work, and yes, he was now walking up the path of the very coffeehouse in which I sat. In itself, this was about as Borgesian a moment as a mere mortal such as myself could ever have, and for that reason, I might think to title this memory, "Borges and I," except that Borges had already written a story called "Borges and I," about an older Borges meeting a younger Borges. And I'm not trying to be imitative here, or cute, though I should add that at the time, I was trying to be imitative, if not cute. At the time, I thought of myself as Borges Jr. I wrote stories full of *significance*, stories in which bizarre things happened. I had no idea why they happened, and no one understood my stories, least of all me, and so in my creative writing classes, students and teachers alike were in awe of me. Thank God, I thought, that writers were never required to explain themselves. Thank God for the subconscious. Even if something seemed utterly without meaning, it might still have *significance* thanks largely to the subconscious and its gentle but insistent way of conning the conscious.

I knew Borges was coming to Bloomington, Indiana. I had simply forgotten when, and so I was taken by surprise. I've always been a bit absent-minded and disorganized, so even though Borges was my literary hero, I had managed to forget the dates of Borges's visit. My professor, Willis Barnstone, had invited Borges to Indiana University. Borges and Willis were great friends, and Willis a translator of Borges's poetry. One of the great ironies of Borges's life was that a man who loved books so much should lose his ability to read them. Over the years, his eyesight worsened to the point of blindness. In 1955, after being appointed the Director of the National Library of Argentina, Borges remarked, "I speak of God's splendid irony in granting me at once 800,000 books and darkness." One of the great literary injustices of the twentieth century was the fact that Borges never won the Nobel Prize. Over the years, Borges had offended the Swedish judges with his remarks about politics, especially his support of rightist regimes in South America. Under the leftist Peron regime, he and his family had been persecuted, his sister thrown in jail, an attempt made to bomb his family home, and he had been appointed poultry inspector for the Buenos Aires municipal market.

Borges himself was always sanguine about being overlooked for the Nobel. "Not granting me the Nobel Prize has become a Scandinavian tradition," Borges remarked once. "Since I was born they have not been granting it to me." The day after Márquez won the Nobel in 1982, the *Boston Globe* quoted novelist A. G. Mojtabai at Harvard, "Every year I look in vain for Borges." She wasn't the only one. But in a way, it's a good thing that Borges never won the Nobel Prize. This oversight simply diminishes the Nobel and reminds us that human judgment is fallible and that the only judgment that matters is that of each individual reader judging each individual writer and what the work on the page means at the moment of contact between reader and writer.

The Runcible Spoon was one of those places where strangers sit with one another at the various tables. My table that day was closest to the door, and that's where Borges and his guide chose to sit, Borges directly across from me. The distance between me and him was perhaps four times (at most) the distance between you and the page you're reading at this moment. You understand that this was my literary hero, that I was not expecting Borges (of course) to wander into the Runcible Spoon that day, nor did I expect that he would sit across from me. When I saw they were heading my way, I quickly threw my copy of *Labyrinths* on the floor beside my chair. I don't know why, but it seemed the thing to do. I felt vaguely embarrassed that I was reading the author who had joined me at the table. And it would have been ridiculous for me to continue reading Borges while Borges sat across from me.

The server took Borges's order quicker than I'd ever seen her move before, and for the next half hour Borges and his guide chatted amiably over a double espresso with lemon rind (Borges) and a Café au lait (guide). My own coffee cup was empty and remained so, only a cold froth at the bottom and around the rim of the cup. I couldn't bring myself to order. I could hardly bring myself to breathe. I wondered what I should say to Borges. I should say something, shouldn't I? But I had no idea what that something should be. I wore a garland of mediocre thoughts. Banal expressions of hero worship tape-looped through my mind. But here was my chance. I could say anything I wanted to Borges if I could only think of what to say, and he would have to acknowledge me. Of course, Borges couldn't see me, or if he did, I only appeared as a vague dark shape, perhaps a potted plant between the table and the window. If he had seen me, he might have said something, some small polite thing to acknowledge that we were sharing the same table. His companion certainly had no intention of acknowledging me. She was with Borges and he was her Borges and I could see from her posture alone, fiercely straight, that she meant to keep him to herself.

What happened happened. I can't alter it now, though at the moment, I wished with all my heart that I could rewind the previous thirty minutes and make something different happen. What happened was this: exactly nothing. The graduate student paid the bill and the two of them got up and left and I looked after them as though I were a ghost watching the living live. Should I say how I felt? Should I spell it out? All I can say is that I knew I would never, not in my wildest imaginings, ever have a chance like this again.

As soon as Borges left, the Runcible Spoon returned to normal—that is, the server resumed her aloof stance between the kitchen and the main floor of the coffeehouse, patrons resumed their studies and conversations, and I retrieved *Labyrinths* off the floor, placed it in my backpack, and drove my moped home.

I know this much. What happened was what should have happened because I've come to understand that this is exactly the relationship of the reader to the writer. The writer vaguely perceives the shape of the reader out there. The reader, barely breathing, wishes there was something to say, anything that would decrease the distance between them. And each is there, directly across the table from the other.

In the Basement of Afflictions

We can never entirely recover what has been forgotten. And this is perhaps a good thing. The shock of repossession would be so devastating that we would immediately cease to understand our longing.
   —Walter Benjamin

The photo on my basement floor appeared one day seemingly out of nowhere, amid the boxes of belongings salvaged from my mother's long life, salvaged from the flood that hit my town two years ago. In that flood I learned that you can live on high ground and still suffer. The water seeps through the walls and soaks books and records and papers and photographs, and what the water doesn't ruin, the mildew will. Ultimately, everything is about letting go, but still we let go reluctantly. Now and then a ruined photo will rise to the surface, still intact in memory. I suppose I could have saved more, but the flood had bad timing. On our way out of town for a year, my wife and I didn't have time for sentimentality. Anything ruined stays ruined. Throw it away, forget about it.

But on our return from our year away, on the basement floor lay an oversized photo, more of a scroll, rolled tightly into itself, so that only its white backside showed. Unrolling it, I recognized it immediately, not as anything with personal meaning but as a cultural artifact. A studio shot for a television show from the fifties, the first reality show, *Queen for a Day*. It's a wide-angle shot of the entire audience with larger photos of the host and cohost inset in front of the anonymous audience.

I stared at the studio shot in befuddlement. What was *Queen for a Day* doing on my basement floor? Obviously, it separated itself somehow from the rest of my mother's boxed belongings, but how, and more importantly, why would she own such a shot, except perhaps as some ironic memento purchased at a thrift store when she was in a giddy mood? But this was more like something I'd buy than she. My mother would have scoffed at the photo, rolled her eyes, and tossed it aside. She hated television. She would have read *Candide* for her understanding of human misery, not watched *Queen for a Day*.

In *Queen for a Day*, the contestants and much of the audience were made up of bedraggled housewives who had suffered more misfortunes than most of us. Their homes had been washed away in hurricanes. Their husbands had left them with nine children to feed. They had been diagnosed with Thrombotic thrombocytopenic purpura and harlequin ichthyosis. They had lost jobs. They had lost teeth. They had lost faith. They had lost the will to live. But they had not lost the desire to appear in front of a live television audience and tell their tales of woe. The audience would clap loudly to determine the most miserable of these women and she would be given as a prize an Amana Radar Range, a refrigerator, a washer and dryer, some consumer good bobbing through the raging flood waters of her life, onto which she would scramble, standing for a moment sure-footed and restored to her rightful place in her ransacked queendom.

Queen for a Day started something in America. It stood for something. It bred. It had nine kids, then twenty.

I should come clean here. I am no expert on *Queen for a Day*. I have never watched a full episode if any still exist, but only snippets, and even these are unwatchable for long. So I cannot say for certain that any one contestant had Thrombotic thrombocytopenic purpura or harlequin ichthyosis or was left with nine children to feed, but these were the general parameters of the show. It celebrated the human spirit in the face of adversity.

I suppose it was doing this still on my basement floor, celebrating the human spirit in the face of adversity. But why? What was it doing on my basement floor?

Actually, I'd known about this show from an early age. The cohost, Jeanne Cagney, was the sister of James Cagney, the legendary Hollywood actor, and also the mother of an elementary school friend of mine. Jeanne Cagney's daughter and I could have made appearances on her mother's show, at least in theory, as I suspect almost everyone in the world could have made an appearance. But we would not have won. My father had died of a heart attack when I was seven. My mother returned to school and she, with the help of my grandmother, supported us. Jeanne Cagney and her husband divorced; my friend, like I, left town, and we did not see each other again for many years, until in middle age when we compared notes on our unhappy childhoods. We had been scarred certainly, but not enough to merit a household appliance.

Perhaps the creators of *Queen for a Day* found their idea for this show in Voltaire's *Candide*. Misery has never been more pleasurable than in Voltaire's hands. In one of my favorite scenes, Cunegonde and the old woman with one butt cheek (the other having been eaten by soldiers) compare notes:

"God grant it," said Cunegonde; "but I have been so horribly unhappy there that my heart is almost closed to hope."

"You complain," said the old woman, "alas! you have not known such misfortunes as mine."

Cunegonde almost broke out laughing, finding the good woman very amusing, for pretending to have been as unfortunate as she.

"Alas!" said Cunegonde, "my good mother, unless you have been ravished by two Bulgars, have received two deep wounds in your belly, have had two castles demolished, have had two mothers cut to pieces before your eyes, and two of your lovers whipped at an auto-da-fé, I do not conceive how you could be more unfortunate than I. Add that I was born a baroness of seventy-two quarterings—and have been a cook!"

But Cunegonde has met her match in the misery contest with the old woman's tale. In fact, every person she encounters has a tale of woe and thinks he or she is the most unfortunate person alive.

After I came across the publicity still for *Queen for a Day*, I placed the photo back on the basement floor where I'd found it. I did this partly out of laziness and partly because this is where the photo lived, on my basement floor. It seemed to belong there. Over the next year, I came upon this photo a dozen times or more, and each time I unrolled it and studied it, wondering why I owned it. Each time I unrolled the scroll, it tore a little more. Each time, I stared at the studio audience in the *Queen for a Day* publicity still for a long while, noting of course that everyone in that photo was most likely long dead. Each had suffered in private, no studio audience to hear their last breaths. How many had died lingering, painful deaths? How many had died sudden deaths? What minority had died peaceful deaths or even now walked among the living?

A few months ago, I came upon it again and unrolled it for a look. I still had no idea why my mother would carry around such a thing. But this time as my eyes roved the studio audience, two people separated themselves from the rest. They sat in the front row, their faces so clear I don't know how I ever missed them: my grandmother Ida and my half sister Nola. Both of them were long since dead. Ida had died at the age of ninety in 1981. Her kidneys had failed and my mother, who sat with her in the hospital, reported to me that as she died she had begged to be brought to her porch where she could see her garden and feel the sun on her face.

Instantly, I had some context for the photo. My sister was eleven or so here, well before the onset of her illness. She had never known her father, who, after finding out that my mother was pregnant, abandoned her. My grandmother had taken Nola on a trip out West to Disneyland. Apparently, they had also visited *Queen for a Day* and watched an episode taped. The photo was snapped as a souvenir to be sold to people who buy such things. My grandmother was one such person. To her, *Queen for a Day* would have been the perfect diversion. A widow for over thirty years by then, her husband had died in his early thirties of an aneurysm and she had supported a large extended family through the Depression on a meager teacher's salary. But by this time in her life, she was quite comfortable if not wealthy. She would have made a terrible contestant on the show. She had both her butt cheeks. She had not been ravished by Bulgars. But there were things that happened in her life, that happen in anyone's life, that she never would have shared, that she would have brought to the grave.

I had always envied my sister this trip, which happened well before my birth. She kept a diary of her adventures but had not mentioned this show, which probably horrified her, or at least confused her. When I was ten or so, I broke the lock and read of teacup rides and other fantasies. I felt cheated. Why had my grandmother taken Nola to Disneyland and not me? Didn't I deserve rewards?

Staring at the picture again, as if for the first time, I saw my dead grandmother and sister from the perspective of the person taking the photograph, from the perspective of one of the contestants. My grandmother smiled. My sister looked curious. I almost felt compelled to tell them something of my life, to fill them in on everything they had missed.

www.ingramcontent.com/pod-product-compliance
Lightning Source LLC
Chambersburg PA
CBHW060244030726
47493CB00025B/2210